Deer Aint Peggy

Deer Aint Peggy
Letters of Advice and Life's Observations from a 14-year-old Basset Hound

Sherlock P. Blanchard

2008

Deer Aint Peggy

TABLE UV CONTENTS

ACKNOWLEDGEMENTS

Thanks to my human friends and relatives who liked my letters so much. Ah'm glad U like to laugh! Ah M alsew glad U encouraged me to put the letters together to make this hear book.

Thanks to Bob for takin me on all uv them long walks where ah did most uv mah thinking about whut to put in those letters. And thanks to Bob fer helpin me to keep mah stories straight en fer helping me to put thuh letters in thuh rite sequence. Also, thanks to Bob fer showin me how to spell "Acknowledgements" up there at the top of the page en fer not gettin on to me too much about how I choose to spell things—the creative freedom has been wonderful.

Last, but not least, I am thankful fer all uv the humans en animals in mah life. I have had a *great* life.

- Sherlock P. Blanchard

To Jan, Aint Peggy, Aint Charleen and Granny—who love me—no matter whut.

- Sherlock

INNERDUCTION

We ain't been innerduced yet. My name iz Sherlock P. Blanchard. The P. iz fer Perry, but you can just call me Sherlock. So hello en howdy-do. Ah am a 14-year-old Basset Hound, en ah am a writer en philosopher. Oh yeah, ah live with Bob en Jan. Walker en Martha live with them too. They iz Bob en Jan's kids.

This here iz a book uv letters that ah have sent to my human relatives en frends over the years (the letters, not the book). Everbuddy kept tellin me how they iz reel interestin en funny en all like that, en ah ought to publish them. Jan sez they are letters but they are also short stories.

I hope you ain't put off by my modern way uv spellin. My rules are reel simple. If it sounds right when you pernounce it, then it iz spelt right. Sew there might be times when you have to read a phrase er a sentence out loud to git my meanin. Ah also ain't afraid uv no slang words like a lot uv English teachers ah know. They say it iz ignorance. Ah say it iz regional dialect witch ought to be preserved, otherwise we iz all goin to end up soundin like a bunch uv TV news reporters.

I will tell you right now that ah don't put no "g" at the end uv words like "going, doing, spelling." Ah don't talk like that; so ah don't rite like that. Ah thank ah would ruther hear fingernails scrape a blackboard than hear people pernounce that "g" at the end uv a word.

They iz a Glossary uv what Bob calls mah more innovative expressions en spellins in the back uv the book. **And** on people's names, if there is a footnote lookin thingie at the end of their name this is called uh endnote, en those notes are way at the end of the book after the Glossary and they explain who the people are. Ah wanted to make em footnotes but the publisher come down on me purty hard about this en made me put em at the end. Sorry about that.

I like people uh hole lot. Ah like communicatin with them. If ah can't be there in person to use my body language en deep meaningful looks, then ah do a hole lot better with letters than ah do on the phone. So here iz them letters ah was talkin about. Ah hope you like em.

There ain't no violence er nudity er sex stuff in this hear book. Uh big part uv my life iz goin outside to do my bidness, if U know whut I mean, en ah talk about that some, but ah don't use no dirty words. However, this ain't no bedtime stories fer little kids sort uv book. "Doo doo" en "wee wee" ain't dirty words is they? They is just about natural thangs U got to do.

Oh yeah, two more things ah gotta clear up: Won: If you R uh mean person er dog er utherwise need to be anonymous, ah changed yore name. Now, if we ain't never met and you come acrost yore name in here, it iz a pure-eyed old accident that yore name iz in here—it iz won uv them made-up names, en ah doan't mean nothin personal by it. Two: If we have met en yore name iz in here it iz because me en Bob like en admire U uh hole lot, even if ah might have embellished yore story uh littul bit.

Welcome to the world uv Sherlock P. Blanchard, Basset Hound.

HOW TO PICK A DOG

Deer Aint Peggy[1],
How R U? Ah M fyne.

Bob gave me your letter en said would ah write you en give you sum advice about gettin a dawg on a count uv ah am a expert on the subject. First off, here are sum tips on how to interpret what sumbody iz sayin when they are tryin to sell you a dawg.

What They Say
What They Mean
Good disposition.
This coward iz even scared uv the mailman.
Alert.
This here dawg barks all night.
Intelligent.
Can slip out uv any collar you put on him
Pedigree.
High strung.
Our favorite uv the litter.
Hope we find sumbody dumb enough to take him.
Good with children.
Chewed the garbage man up last week.
Eats well.
Has been raised on hambooger en steak.
Obedient.
Don't run away when he iz tied up.
Knows lots uv tricks.
Chews the furniture en pees in the house.

Has a good coat.
We can't keep fleas off uv this mutt
Needs a lot uv exercise.
The dawg takes you fer a walk!!!
Is a good watch dawg.
Wants to be frends with everbuddy he sees.
Very frendly.
Wags his tail before he bites you.
Has champion blood lines.
His father was a travelin man.
Has a lot uv potential.
You might git him to come to you when you call if you work on it fer two er three years.
Eager to learn.
Looks at you when you talk to him.
Registered.
Has a criminal record.
Well mannered.
Won't doo-doo in the same room he peed in.

Now, before ah go any further, don't git no cocker spaniel. Ninety percent uv the blond haired ones are called Honey, en the other ten percent are called Buffy. En all the black ones iz called Onyx er Blackie. Well ah tell you, after about ten er twelve generations uv that kind uv name callin en them cocker spaniels iz pure-eyed-old wimps. You will notice this on a count uv they groan a lot. They ain't got the nerve to whine like a real he-man like me.

Oh yeah, another thang. If the dawg ain't got brown-colored eyes, don't git him er her. You ever look at a Husky straight on? They got these weird light colored eyes like gray er green. It'll scare the you-know-what out uv you. They iz this here dawg acrost the street who belongs to Mister Wicker. He iz a Australian sumthin er other (the dawg, not Mister Wicker), en he has one blue eye en one brown eye. He gives me the shivers. Plus he don't talk like no Australian — you know, like "G'day mate" en all like that. He iz prolly a communist spy from Russia er sumthin. If he ever slips up en says "Comrade" er "revolution" er "red" ah am goin straight home en call Senator You-No-Who.

O.K. Now the psychological part — a lot uv people overlook that piece uv it. You got to figure out whether you wont a first-born puppy er one that ain't first born — you know, like number two er three er four in the litter. The first born puppy iz in touch with his thinkin, en one that ain't first born ain't. Take me fer instance — ah was number five. Well ennyhow them uv us that ain't first born iz in touch with our feelins. So, first borns have a real strong sense uv duty en are real serious — you can't tell a first born no jokes. But us second en third, en fourth en what-all borns bein in touch with our feelins are more sensitive en know how to have fun en we really like music en art en cookies.

Oh yeah. Another important consideration: Ears. First make sure your dawg has at least two en that they work. Bob says ah am livin proof that the size uv your ears iz no indication that they work.

I hope this helps you pick out the dawg that's right fer you.

I wished ah was as good at gettin rid uv dawgs on a count uv this here dawg name uv B.D. down the street. Ah asked him what B.D. stood fer en he said "B.D! U wont to make sumthin uv it?" Well ennyhow, ah don't know what kind uv a dawg he is; sew I'll just say don't git no big, yeller haired dawg with a dumb look on their face.

Sounds like y'all have a real nice new home. Ah know what you mean about wishin you had more trees. Ah hate it when you have to walk a long ways before you can pee cause they ain't no trees in your yard. So I'm glad we got them all over the place. Bob likes the shade but he doesn't like the leaves in the gutters, but like ah tell him, "Well Bob," ah say, "everthang has its advantages en its disadvantages. You got to take the good with the bad, the shade with the gutter." I'd git up there en clean them gutters out my ownself, but Bob says ah might fall en land on my face en end up lookin like a bulldog.

Well, take it easy en tell everbuddy hi fer me. Bob en Jan en Walker en Martha say hi too.

Your frend forever,

Sherlock P. Blanchard

BOB GITS STUCK WITH THE SHORT STRAW

Deer Diary,

Guess whut? Well me en Bob iz on a great advenchure! Yep! We have dun come down here to Ocala, Florida where Bob en Jan grew up, en we iz goin on a one week fishin trip at the Oklawaha River in the national forrest with sum uv Bob's old high skool buddies.

Bob sed this might be uh good oppertoonity fer me to start a diary. So here we go en howdy do.

Day I: Well we all piled in Phil K's van with all the campin en fishin en cookin gear en groceries en cold drinks en coolers en ah don't know what all. En we drove out the Daytona highway witch iz named after Daytona don't you know. We didn't go to Daytona. They just call it the Daytona highway on acuz it iz on the way to Daytona. Ah guess if you live in Daytona you call it the Ocala highway. Ah asked Bob what did they call the highway there at Astor Park witch iz half way between Daytona en Ocala, en Bob said since they iz only one highway goin through Astor Park, they prolly call it The Highway.

Well, ennyhow, hear iz the names uv all uv us who iz on this hear trip. Sherlock, Bob, Lloyd D., Phil K., Buddy M. en Unkel Hugh. Ah will tell you all about them tomorrow er the next day, but right now they iz a lot that happened; sew ah got to git that part wrote down.

Ennyhow, we drove out the Daytona Highway, then we got off on a couple county roads, then we got on four er five dirt roads, en finally after about two hours we come to a place out in the middle uv nowhere with a river runnin through it, witch iz called the Oklawaha River. They iz sum peepul who found out in sum histery book it used to be spelled Ocklawaha en they iz tryin to git it changed. Ah figure the guy who wrote that their histery book couldn't spell too good, en U no my feelins about them silent letters, sew ah figure that there "C" ought to be invisible, en it ought to stay Oklawaha.

Ennyhow, when we got out, Uncle Hugh said, "Yep, Sherlock, we iz in the wilderness. They ain't a phone er a CoCola machine fer 30 miles, witch iz why ah brought all a them Co-Colas." Ah asked him how he was goin to keep them cold since he didn't bring no ice.

Well, after Uncle Hugh done got back with the ice, all the old high skool buddies had a discussion about the cookin duties. So Lloyd said, "How about this? We all draw straws. The guy who gets the short straw has to cook en clean the dishes while the rest uv us fish. Now he will do the cookin en cleanin until sumbuddy complains about the cookin. The first man who complains about the cookin takes over the cookin en cleanin duties, en sew on." Well, everbuddy said that sounded like a good idea, en they drew straws. Wouldn't you know it, old Bob drew the short straw.

So Bob fixed lunch. Baloney sandwiches, stewed tomatoes, grits en CoColas. Everbuddy thought it was real good. They went down to the river to fish while Bob washed the pots en pans en plates en all.

That night Bob cooked up sum steaks en collard greens en corn. Strawberry Koolaid to drink. Everbuddy thought it was real good. They all sat around the campfire playin cards en braggin about the fish they caught that day while Bob washed the pots en pans en plates en all.

Day 2: Bob has done figured out ain't nobody goin to complain about his cookin on acuz they don't want to have to take over the cookin duties. So fer breakfast Bob served cold coffee, scorched scrambled eggs en cold, lumpy grits with too much salt on them. Everbuddy sat down en ate in silence. They all looked kind uv shocked, but ain't nobody said a word. They ain't about to complain. Everbuddy except Bob got up from breakfast en went down to the river to fish. Bob washed the pots en pans en plates en all.

About lunch time Bob was gettin desperate. Fried fish, burnt to a crisp. Cold coffee with salt in it. Collard greens with dirt mixed in. Everbuddy ate. Not a word. Not a whimper. Ah wouldn't want to play poker with none uv these guys on acuz they know how to keep a straight face. They all went fishin. Bob was stuck with washin all the dishes en cleanin up.

That afternoon ah decided to take a walk. Bob was in a pretty bad mood; sew ah figured ah would just git away fer awhile. I'd been wanderin around a pretty good while, when ah came upon a cow pasture. Just inside the fence ah found a nice ripe cow plopper. So ah dropped my shoulder in it en then rolled over on my back right in the middle uv it (the cow plopper, not my back) real good.

When ah got back to camp Bob said, "Sherlock! What iz that smell! You stink! Sherlock, you ought to know better than to roll around in a cow plopper! You ain't sleepin in my tent to-night." En then Bob got this funny look on his face, en he said, "Sherlock, show me where that cow pasture is." En Bob took a bucket along. When we got to the cow pasture Bob picked up sum cow ploppers. He brought em back to camp en made a cow manure pie.

Supper time. Soggy fried fish, loaded with pepper. Warm CoColas with pepper in them. Dirt in the grits. Everbuddy ate in silence. Then Bob served up that there cow manure pie. Old Buddy M. was the first one to take a little bite. He spit it out right quick en said, "Yuck! Patooey! Patooey! Patooey! This here iz cow manure!" En Bob said, "Ah Ha!" En then Buddy said, real quick like, he said "But good!" Then they was this big debate about how the rules don't say you got to eat it, you just don't have to complain about it. It was four against one. Ah stayed out uv it. Bob lost.

Up till then ah ain't never seen a grown man cry. En ah am sorry to say it was Bob who was the first one ah ever did see. Ah went fer a walk. Bob washed the dishes.

The end.

FORD FANS: FOUR. SHIVVERLAY FANS: ONE

Deer Diary,

How R U? Ah M fyne.

Well, it iz day number four uv our big fishin en campin trip advenchure at the Oklawaha River.

On day number three everbuddy got tired uv eatin Bob's sorry food, plus they was worried about cow manure showin up in their beans er collard greens er sumthin; sew they switched off on the cookin chores. Bob has been real happy ever since.

It iz rainin today, sew we iz all sittin in the tent en Bob's high skool buddies iz all tellin stories on each other. Uncle Hugh, who iz Jan's brother, told the ones about how Bob wasn't no good at doin pushups in football practice en how another time they was on a canoe trip down Juniper Creek en a snake slid off a limb into the canoe. This iz about the third time ah heard Unkle Hugh tell that there snake story. Each time the snake gets bigger en Bob jumps higher. First time he told it Bob jumped in the water. This time Bob jumped clear out on the bank.

Lloyd D. en Phil K. en Buddy M. en Bob all worked together when they was in high school at the Silver Springs Soda Shop. They worked out there on weekends en durin the summer. Actually Buddy wasn't in high skool. He was older then en was the manager uv the place. Hiz wife is Ruth en she iz from Pennsylvania, but she ain't nothin like a Yankee — she iz reel nice. Bob says Buddy iz the hardest workin man he ever knew except fer Unkel Joe; sew Buddy set a real good example. Bob said he didn't stand a chance back then bein sandwiched in between

Buddy settin a good example, en everbuddy always tellin Bob what a hard worker his older brother Joe was.

Well they all had a whole bunch uv funny Yankee tourist stories to tell. The one ah like the most iz where this here lady from New York got all het up about Ross Allen's Reptile Institute cuttin one leg off uv each one uv the flamingos to keep them from flyin away. Actually, the flamingos rest one leg at a time by tuckin them up under their bodies.

Lloyd went on to become a Marine jet pilot in Vietnam. En then he finished college with a straight 'A" average. He iz now got a mobil home bidness in Chiefland en does real good. He married Miss Linda, en they have a beautiful home on the Suwannee River. Bob says Lloyd iz the best dove shot he ever did see, en iz a real gentleman. He does a good job uv catchin them redfish en speckled sea trout too. When Bob en Jan en Walker en Martha iz visitin relatives in Ocala en Belleview en Leesburg en Eustis, Bob en Lloyd usually git together en go fishing on the Gulf coast at Homosassa, Suwannee, Wacasassa er Cedar Key.

Phil went into the wholesale grocery bidness en has his own bidness now. He lives on Little Lake Weir en married Betty, whose sister married uh cousin uv Jan's, sew we iz related. Bob en Phil usually git together at the Coffee Kettle Restaurant there in Ocala en have fried grouper en French fries. Bob says they put ketchup on thangs en catch up on things.

Unkel Hugh en Bob go way back to junior hi skool days. They even played on thuh same Babe Ruth baseball team. Unkel Hugh en Aint Peggy live in Texas now where Unkel Hugh builds beautiful homes en Aint Peggy iz a big upitty-up in thuh Texas State Hospital system. We allus try to git to Florida at thuh same time when we visit Granny.

Before we went on this trip Bob showed me pictures uv Lloyd en Phil in his high skool annual, en it was interestin to see

Uncle Hugh's picture. Uncle Hugh had as his fondest memory, "Bein NEC champs," the NEC bein the name uv the conference. Lloyd's fondest memory was the homecomin victory over Gainesville High School.

I noticed Bob's fondest memory was "All the fine teachers at Ocala High School." Ah asked Bob what made him put that, en he said, "Sherlock, you don't burn no bridges before you git to them. Ah didn't exactly have Mr. Bell's Senior English en Coach Bucha's[2] Advanced Math class made in the shade. Ah figured anythang ah could do to grease the skids was icin on the cake. Plus, since ah tore my knee up playin football in the 10th grade, ah didn't git to play no more football er basketball er nothin; sew ah couldn't say my fondest memory was scorin a game winnin touchdown in the last two seconds uv the conference championship er nothin like that."

I looked up Jan's fondest memory en it said, "Basketball, teachers, en friends." Boy, she had all the bases covered. Ah notice back then she put the comma before the and. Ah asked her why she didn't mention Bob as a fond memory, en she said, "Sherlocky wocky, back then ah was just the sister uv one uv Bob's buddies, namely Hugh; sew Bob didn't even notice me. We didn't start goin together until we were in college en Hugh was at a different college over in Mississippi."

I asked Bob why didn't he notice Jan in high school, en Bob said, "I noticed her plenty. But she was Hugh's sister. Ah would a been em-bare-ussed to go out with her." Sum people ain't got no brains when they are in high skool. Bob must a been right there in the middle uv that pack. Ah sure am glad he got a whole lot smarter when he got to college.

Phil's fondest memory was "December 12th." Ah asked Bob iz that when Phil kissed his first girl, en Bob said, "Nope. That there was the day Phil got his driver's license. Phil wasn't inter-ested in no girls back then. He was like Walker. He loved cars."

I learned that Phil was a Ford fan. Then ah took a poll around the tent. Sort uv a tent pole. Haw! Haw! Haw! You know how it is. Early in life you make THE two critical choices: 1. Are you a Ford fan er a Shivverlay fan? 2. Are you a CoCola drinker er a Pepsi drinker? Everbuddy said they was a CoCola drinker, but this was because Buddy used to have a CoCola de-livery route. In fact, he had the largest CoCola delivery route in the entire U.S. of A., en that's uh fact! Talk about workin hard, when he left the CoCola company to go to work fer Mr. Thomas at the Silver Springs Soda Shop, why they had to break his CoCola route up into two full time routes on acount uv no-body else could git it all done by theirselves.

Now the big choice: Ford fan er Shivverlay fan? Uncle Hugh iz a Ford fan on acount uv his en Jan's daddy whose name was Pop was a mechanic en the maintenance manager uv Ocala Motors witch iz the Ford place. Bob iz always been a Ford fan, but he ain't real religious about it. Oh sure he says he ain't never bought no Shivverlay, but his pickup truck he ain't never goin to part with iz a GMC. Ah done said Phil was a Ford fan. Buddy iz a Ford fan. This leaves Lloyd. He iz a Shivverlay fan! He just goes on en on about all the great Shivvy trucks he has had, en next thang you know everbuddy iz tryin to outdo one another en its my Ford this en my Shivvy that. We got Fords pullin semi tractor trailers out uv a swamp, en Shivvy's pushin a Sherman tank to git it jump started, en ah don't know what all. Ain't nobody changed their minds, but they all had a intense time talkin about it, kind uv like a Babtist en uh Pentecostal Holiness arguin about who iz goin to Heaven en who ain't. Everbuddy did agree on one thang. They all hated their arch enemy Gainesville High School, en even to this day ain't none uv them will wear anythang with purple on it on a count uv that was Gainesville's skool color.

Day 5: Well, it iz still rainin; sew everbuddy decided to go back to Ocala to the pool hall in the back uv the barber shop next to the Marion Theater en shoot pool fer the rest uv the day en then go home.

On the way to the pool hall we all sang A Hundred Bottles uv Beer on the Wall, except we started at forty bottles on acount uv we never would a got all uv them bottles off the wall — Phil wasn't willin to drive that slow.

We iz in the pool hall now. Everbuddy iz chewin big wads uv bubble gum en drinkin CoColas, en Unkel Hugh iz about to put the eight ball in the corner pocket.

The End.

IF YOU AIN'T GONNA ROLL IN IT, YOU PROLLY DON'T WANT TO STEP IN IT

Deer Unkel Buddy[3],

How R U? Ah M fyne. Jan iz fyne. Bob iz fyne. Walker iz fyne. Martha iz fyne. We iz all fyne.

Aint Charleen says you are doin a physical fitness thing where you walk en jog. Well, ah figure ah can give you sum advice about that on acuz ah take Bob on a walk ever mornin. Actually, Bob walks en ah jog — that way we keep up with each other.

Now, uh, sum uv these here tips is, uh, shall we say, delicate matters, but you bein a vetenaryen en all, ah figure ah can speak freely. So here goes:

The first thang you got to learn iz how to pace yourself. What you do, see, iz seek out opportunities to stop fer a couple seconds ever three er four minutes by wee-weein on prominent terrain features like mailbox posts en road sign posts en empty beer cans.

To help open up your breathin passages, when you come acrost anythang rank, just stop en drop your right shoulder in it en roll on over on it on your back. The best rank thangs to roll in iz cow manure en raccoon ploppers, but seein as how you live in Miami, they ain't many cows er raccoons; sew keep yore eyes peeled fer alligator poop en flamingo doo-doo. If'n you ain't goin to roll in it, then you prolly don't want to step in it. You can just git down en sniff it real good.

Now, if'n you stick to the pavement en off uv the grass, you won't have to clip your toenails no more, on a count uv the pavement will keep your toenails wore down.

To keep cool, you got to keep your mouth about half way open en hang your tongue out uv one side — it don't matter witch side.

Also, be careful jumpin over shrubs when you are runnin. Your whatcha callems — well, they hang down further than you think, sew watch out they don't git caught er banged up on sumthin. Ah hit mine on a stingin nettle one time. Thought ah would die!

Always walk up hill en run down hill, en just let yourself go on the down hill part. Just throw your head back en let your ears flop back in the breeze over your shoulders.

And another thang. Don't let it bother you that you have to doo-doo more than once when you go walkin en joggin. Ah figure once ever ten minutes iz about right. If'n nature calls more than that, consult your physician.

Me en Bob iz always arguin about who has it tougher when we go on a walk. He says he has got it tougher cause he only has two legs en ah got four. Ah say ah got it tougher cause my legs ain't as long as his, en another thang — he ain't bein drug around on no leash. Then he says, "Yeah, but you only weigh 43 pounds en ah weigh a whole bunch more than that." This iz where he always wins the argument.

Well, sew much fer the walkin en joggin tips.

That's about it. Oh yeah, Walker was inducted into the National Honor Society recently, en Martha made the 'A' honor roll this time around.

Well, it iz time to go outside en wee-wee. Bob always goes outside with me, but the only time he wee-wees out there iz at night. Ah don't see how he holds it all day.

Good luck with that walkin en joggin bidness.

Your frend forever,

Sherlock

SHERLOCK P. BLANCHARD, COMPUTER MAN

Deer Aint Peggy,

How are you? I am fine.

I am writin you on this hear personal computer what Sandy Claws brought us on Christmas day. It is real interestin. PC is what computer men like me en Walker calls a Personal Computer. Ennyhow the PC has got this thing called Spell Checker. Whooooooeeeeee! What'll they think of next?

Well ennyhow, I got all finished with the typin and then I hit that there Spell Checker key. The screen went blank and the lights went out in Georgia, which is pretty good considerin we live in North Carolina. I must have had 40 words spelled wrong!

Walker said, "That ain't so bad Sherlock. I did a word count check on your letter, and they is about 200 words here. You got 80% right. That would even be a "C" in Mr. Bell's English class."

Well, with this Spell Checker thing I figured I could go for a "A." But I did the Spell Check stuff up to this point, en I just got plum wore out makin all a them changes. I also couldn't bring myself to put the "g" at the end of those words like "makin" en "interestin." It just makes me shudder to hear that "g." Anyhow, the rest of this here letter ain't been corrected. You are gettin a "B" letter, but that don't mean I don't love you or nothin like that.

How to reed the rest uv this here lettur.

By Sherlock P. Blanchard

I got one spellin rule: If it sounds right it iz spelt right. For example, *and* iz pernounced *en*, sew that iz how ah spell it. Same way: *or* iz pernounced *er*, sew that iz how ah spell it.

Ritin en Readin style rules: If you ain't ritin like you talk, you are bein uppity. This means two thangs:

1. If ah put them "g's" on the end uv words endin with *in*, then you wood think ah am a Yankee. Yankees say thangs like walking, talking, eating. But ah say walkin, talkin, eatin.

2. If'n you have trubbel readin what ah rote, then read it out loud, en you can hear what ah am sayin. Doin this works reel well, especially if'n you R sittin er standin near strangers.

There iz one exsepshun to mah rite-like-U-talk rule. Even though I pernounce it "assed," Bob makes me rite it "asked" whenever ah M askin about sumthin.

This PC don't give you no slack. Here ah am, clackin away on the keybored, reel careful to keep my paws at the proper keybored puzishun. Let me tell you! It iz reel hard fer me to stretch my pinkie up to the Q en the P keys. One time one uv my toe nails got jammed in between the K en the L key, en ah was pushin en pullin en howlin en the old PC was goin KLKLKLKLKLK L KLKLKLKLKLKL KLKL KKK LLL en then my toe nail come a loose (from the keybored, not from my paw).

Ennyway, ah typed this hear letter en it was reel hard on a count uv sittin up straight in this chair iz a strain on my back. Ah give up on all uv this fancy standard puzishun fer your paws on the keybored en just got down to the old hunt-and-peck method. That way, ah could rest my left foot on the desk en just type with my right index toe. This iz a whole lot easier on my back. Ah am thinkin about sendin this information in to one a them health magazines so people will know how to type better en impruve their achin back at the same time.

It was good to see you en Unkel Hugh en Charlton en Roger[4] right after Christmas. It was the bestest present ah ever got.

Everbuddy here was sayin after you all left that they wished y'all could a stayed a hole lot longer.

Also everbuddy said they was glad y'all were hear while J.B. en Lois were here, sew everbuddy got a chance to visit. J.B. en Lois[5] took off the day y'all left en they went to Ohio. Ah asked Bob was Ohio in Texas near where you live, en he said, "No. Ohio was a couple counties over." Now you ain't gonna believe this, but Bob says where J.B. en Lois are goin in Ohio they iz a big lake called Erie, en it iz bigger than any uv them Texas lakes! Ah figure Bob iz just jokin on acuz Roger done told me ain't no lakes bigger than Texas lakes.

We got this here neighbor dog name uv Shane. He iz a German Shepurd , en he iz a little older than me; sew ah got to have respect. Shane thinks he iz the king uv the neighborhood, en he comes over to the house walkin reel slow like, en he don't smile er jump around er even wag his tail much. He iz just checkin thangs out don't you see. Well ennyhow, ah don't give him no trubbel, en we git along pretty good. Don't tell nobuddy, but when Shane ain't lookin, ah go over en do a nummer two in his yard. Then ah do a nummer one on his mailbox post.

Well, ah ain't been any place interestin to tell you about lately. Oh yeah, Bob en me went up to the lake witch iz about three miles from the house. Bob says don't forget we go sum place ever mornin. Ah take Bob fer a walk. Ah am trainin Bob to come up to my standard. When we git back from one uv our walks, Bob iz wheezin en groanin en moanin en ah ain't even broke into a sweat yet. Durin the week we walk about two miles ever mornin, en we do up to four miles on Saturday en on Sunday. They iz lots uv woods around, en we walk in the woods. This iz when ah do mah best thinkin.

Well, that's about it on this here end.

Bob en Jan say they hope everbuddy will come fer another visit reel soon.

Luv forever,

Sherlock

WHY DO THEY CALL EM HAMBOOGERS?

Deer Aint Charleen[6],

How R U? Ah M fyne.

Guess what. I'm goin to be in Martha's Biology report. She had to take pictures uv 20 livin organisms en write a report about each one. En ah am one uv them! She says ah am the smartest livin organism she iz writin about next to the cats en a horse en a fern house plant.

Walker iz doin pretty good. He had the flu fer about ten days right near the Christmas holiday. He missed a lot uv school, en has been busy catchin up on his homework. Except since we got this here PC me en Walker been sharin it a pretty good bit. Walker wrote this program that draws the Olympic circles on the PC screen one by one. En while the circles are showin up the PC plays the Olympic song, just like on the TV. Walker programmed the song part too.

Well, was Sandy Claws good to you? He brung me a hambooger patty rubber chew toy witch looks like a hambooger, but tastes like rubber.

I wonder why hamboogers iz called that on a count uv they ain't no ham en they ain't no boogers in them. Bob says the word iz actully spelt hamburger, but we pernounce it hambooger.

Where was I? Oh yeah, so since the thang tasted like rubber ah give it to Tubby en Tweetums in the dinin room where they iz a wood floor. They play hockey puck with it. Ah also got one uv them orange glow-in-the-dark collars.

Jan says she hopes the Christmas package fer Spencer and Leigh[7] got there OK.

Jan iz treatin me real good. She got a microwave oven fer Christmas, en she iz havin a pretty good time with it. She does a real good job uv warmin up leftovers fer me in the MW (I figure MW iz what a computer man like myself should call a microwave oven). Jan does a whole lot uv other kinds uv cookin in the MW. Bob fixes me hot dogs in the MW when Jan ain't around.

I guess you know that Granny[8] iz still here. Well she is. Bob en Jan en Martha en Walker seem real happy about it. To tell you the truth, Granny don't git on to me sew much any more; sew ah am glad she can stay a spell.

Well, you remember them two kitties that live here? They are about five months old now, en they are startin to go outside. Jan en Walker en Martha call them Tubby en Tweetums. Bob calls them Cooter en Earl after these two little boys what use to live over at the Roberts house en they was always gettin into trubble. Oh yeah, Jan also calls them the terrorists (the kitties, not the two little boys) when they git into trubble, like knockin a lamp off the table.

Old Brother, Martha's cat, iz doin pretty good. He don't like Tweetums en Tubby too much, but he tolerates em. Mainly if they try to play with him, old Bro hisses at them en gives them the old one—two with his right paw, but ah notice that Bro don't never stick his claws out. Ennyhow, the terrorists think Bro iz real interestin en nice, en they bother him whenever they are not too busy racin around en wrestlin each other.

Jan says Bro purrs like a semi truck goin up a slow hill en Tubby en Tweetums purr like a lawn mower cuttin tall grass.

This here North Carolina iz a pretty nice place. Everbuddy iz settled in hear pretty good. Ah don't mind tellin you that when ah was movin hear, ah thought North Carolina was in sum foreign country like New York er Chicago. Ah was real worried about havin to learn a foreign language. Boy howdy was ah relieved. Peeple here talk more like me than ah do.

I asked Bob were we goin to have a woman vetenaryen here like you, en Bob said, "Sherlock, they ain't no woman vet like Aint Charleen. She iz Jan's sister, en she iz the best woman vet they is. Come to think uv it, Uncle Buddy iz tied with Dr. Hines[9] fer the best man vet they is, but we will find a good vetenaryen fer you."

The search iz on. Ah got interviews scheduled through next Friday.

Well, that's about it on this here end.

Luv forever,

Sherlock

YOU AIN'T GONNA BELIEVE WHUT DOCTOR WILSON DID WITH THE THERMOMETER!

Deer Aint Nita[10],

How R U? Ah M purty good.

Bob took me to the vet. His name iz Doctor Wilson, except he lets me call him Doc fer short. Well, ennyhow, ah went there fer my general all around check-up en shots. Right off the bat, Doc gets out this here thang called a rectal thermometer, en you won't believe what he done with it! Not only that, he left it in there about three er four minutes!

That ain't the worst uv it. When we got there, Bob starts walkin me around en around in Doc's little yard, en Bob kept sayin, "Come on Sherlock. Doo-doo." Well, after he said it about twenty times, ah got the general idea, en sew ah went pretty good. Now, you ain't goin to believe this, but the next thang ah know, Bob iz down there pickin up one uv my ploppers with uh popsicle stick en puttin it in a little paper cup. Then he marches right in to the Doc's office en gives this here doo-doo in the paper cup to Doc's helper. Her name iz Margaret, en she says, "Why thank you." just like Bob had give her sum flowers er sumthin!

Well, after the rectal thermometer ordeal en the doo-doo in the cup, Doc gets real mean. He pulls out this here surrenge with a needle about a foot long en a square point en he jabs that sucker right in my left front leg, right above my ankle. Bob says they ain't no such a thang as a surrenge with a one foot needle with a square point. He says it was only about two inches long en it had a real sharp point. Well, ennyhow, Doc jabs that thang into me en sucks out sum uv my blood! Then about that time Margaret come through the door en says, "Sherlock iz got hook worms en tape worms!" She said it like she was real proud uv me, sew ah wagged my tail fer her a little bit.

Well, if that wasn't enough, Doc give me this here shot under my skin between my shoulder blades. Then he gets this here other surrenge with a invisible needle on the end uv it. Ah know it was invisible, cause ah couldn't see it. Ennyhow, he grabs my nose en says, "Open wide Sherlock." Well, ah figure he was goin to jab me in the tonsils er my punchin bag hangey-down thang at the top uv my throat. Well, ah give him a little trubble over that let me tell you. En then he yelled at me. "Sherlock! Be still er ah will unscrew your belly button en your hind legs will fall off!" Bob says he ain't said no such a thang — Doc was just bein firm with me. Huh! What does Bob know? He was standin there all uv this time from the rectal thermometer right on up to this, en all the time he iz sayin, "It's Okay buddy. Take it easy. You're a good boy." Easy fer him to say. He ain't gettin jabbed. Well, ennyhow, this here invisible needle wasn't no needle at all. Doc just squirted sum uv this white stuff in my mouth. He said it was to kill the hookworms en the tape worms.

Well, then Bob starts tellin thangs on me. First he showed Doc my three warts. Next he starts tellin Doc about how my teeth must bother me cause when ah eat dry dog food, ah whimper a little bit sumtimes. Ah was EM-BARE-USSED! Then he got to tellin on me about how ah shiver sumtimes in the house, en whine a little bit. Well, right away, Doc starts talkin about this fellow name uv Arthur Itis, who ah don't even know, en how he ought to take a couple uv little assburns ever mornin en evenin. Well, even though Doc iz a veterinarian, it iz illegal fer him to be givin out prescriptions to people, but ah guess it was all right since this here Arthur Itis wasn't actually present en Doc was only talkin about assburns en not no real drugs like Ex-Lax er Dristine.

Lets see, where was I? Oh yeah, this here shiverin bidness. Ah tell you why ah am shiverin. It iz on a count uv Scamper. She iz this cute little miniature Schnauzer who lives acrost the street. Well, she wants to git married! Real bad. That's enough to give a old bachelor like me the shivers. She puts me through this about ever six months. She iz real interestin en nice en all like that, but married? Uh uh. Why, what if we got married en had kids. First off, she iz real cute, en ah am sort uv handsome if ah do say sew my own self, but what if the kids come out with her body en my ears, er my body, but her ears. Ah mean it would give anybody the shivers.

Oh yeah, Bob had to go to the dentist the other day with a tooth that was botherin him. He come back en said, "Sherlock, they IS such a thang as a surrenge with a one foot needle with a square point on the end, cause that there dentist used it on me!" Ah asked Bob did the dentist have a rectal thermometer too? Haw! Haw! Haw!

Well, that's about it on this here end.

Luv,

Sherlock

IF IT IZ SILENT WHEN YOU SAY IT, IT OUGHT TO BE INVISIBLE WHEN YOU RITE IT

Deer Aint Peggy,

How R U? Ah M fyne.

Ah been thinkin a lot lately about how they ain't many trees out there in Texas where you live, en ah have come up with a new rule fer spellin that would save the trees en make life a whole lot easier fer everbuddy. Well it wouldn't make it any easier fer the Russians on a count uv they got differnt alphabet en all. Ennyhow, here iz the new rule: If it iz silent when you say it, it ought to be invisible when you write it. Fer ezzampul, with the new way uv spellin, we could save a hole bunch uv letters when we eat a donut, we could drop the "h" off the front uv "hour" and the "e" off uv "minute." We mow the grass with a mor (drop out the "we" part in the middle). We could drink sweet ice te. We could git them "h's" out the middle uv "wy" en "wen." Just think uv all the paper this could save! We could prolly cut twinny pages out uv ever book, en the newspapers could be ten percent smaller. This would take less paper, en paper comes from trees; sew we would be savin the trees, don't you see.

I wrote to Senator You-No-Who about makin this a constitutional amendment er sumthin er other, but ah ain't heard back from the Senator just yet. Bob says the Senator iz prolly too busy with politics en all the other ticks to work on this spellin idea right now. Plus they ain't no tax on trees, sew this here idea wouldn't save no taxes. Well, maybe they ought to put a tax on silent letters, en that would make em invisible real quick.

Bob got me to thinkin about this new spellin rule. When Bob has a little too much root beer to drink, he gets to talkin about how he pitched a no hits, no walks, no errors baseball game the openin day uv Little League season when he was twelve en how when he was ten he could have been a world champion speller.

See, win Bob wuz in thuh forth grade, he reperzented his class in a spellin bee in front uv the hole school. He was up aginst forth graders from other classes en alsew aginst fifth en sixth graders. Wel, Bob did reel good, en they was only four speller competishion kids left en Miz Walters, she was callin out the words, she sed, "Bob, spell frend." En Bob spelt it f-r-e-i-n-d, en awl thuh kids in Bob's class clapped, on a count uv they new that was right, but Miz Walters sed, "Childrun! Be quiet! That iz wrong. Bob, sit down. U iz out. Mary Lou, honey, spell frend."

Now Mary Lou Smith had staid inside fer three weekends in a row en didn't go outside en play sew she could go thew the dickshunerry sevun times spellin ever werd. Meanwhile, Bob en all the other kids, they was outside playin baseball en rollin in the dirt en ridin thir bicyccles, en havin a real good time on them three weekends Mary Lou was inside studyin them words. Where was I? Oh yeah. Back at the spellin bee. Miz Walters iz sayin, "Mary Lou, honey, spell frend." Wel Mary Lou sed, reel calm sorta like, she sed, "Frend. F-R-I-E-N-D. Frend." En then Mary Lou went on to win the competishun on the werd antidis-establishmentarianism er sum other easy werd like that.

Oh shore, shore, ah no U R jest uh klukkin yore tung en sayin to yoreseff, "I" befoar "E" essept after sumthin er uther. Wel, lets just take the modern approach to this here prollem. First off, U thow ouwt thuh dang "I" on a count uv it iz silent! This solves that dumb "I" before "E" rule, en U just spell it F-

R-E-N-D, en Mary Lou coulda been outside ridin her bicyccle with her frends all that time!. Ah rest mah case.

Yore frend furevvur,

Sherlock

AIN'T NOBODY APPRECIATES MY WEE-WEEIN NOWHERE

Deer Unkel Joe en Aint Bobbye Nann[II],

How R U? Ah M fyne.

Well, ah just got my ears washed en doctored up by Bob, en it iz Saturday night, en ah ain't got no date er nothin, sew ah thought I'd write you this here letter. Oh yeah, my dang ears iz givin me a little trubbel, but the vet said it ain't nothin serious like rabies er a brain tumor er nothin like that.

Well, everbuddy iz doin pretty good. We are all ready fer spring — especially me. The last time Bob give me a bath, ah lost a whole bunch uv hair; sew ah figure that's my winter coat — er else I'm a goin bald. Ah notice that the flowers are even ready fer spring — they just tryin real hard to bud.

Well, old Walker done adopted that there Mustang that Bob got all fixed up. It shore iz purty. All the mechanical stuff like the engine en water pump en brakes en all like that has done been completely rebuilt en all uv the insides where the seats en head liner en dash board, en carpets iz all been redone, en this here fellow in town done put the prettiest paint job on the old Mustang you ever did see. Ennyhow, old Walker done put the boat outside the garage en that's where the Mustang stays. Jan sewed together sum sheets en Walker covers up the Mustang with them ever night. Ah guess he don't want it to git cold er nothin. Ah bet if he could figure out a way to drive that there Mustang inside the house, he would do it. Ennyhow, Walker takes better care uv the Mustang than U take care uv yore cars,

Unkel Joe. Now, ah know that don't hardly seem possible, but he does. He won't even let me git near the dang car — he says, "Sherlock! Get away from there! En don't you pee on them tires ever again, er you are dead meat!" En then he hit me! Yep, with a bull whip en tire chains, en a two by four, en a baseball bat, en a Russian Army belt! Bob says that ain't true, Walker just pushed me away from the car a little bit. Well ennyhow, before ah pee on them Mustang tires, ah look around real good to see if Walker iz around first.

I peed on Jan's potted plants the other day. She had em out in the yard to git sum fresh air en sunshine, en ah heard her say she needed to water en fertilize em. Sherlock at your service. Hike a hind leg. Unfortunately, Jan caught me waterin the third plant. Well, ah ain't goin to tell you what all Jan said to me, cause you wouldn't believe no lady could talk like that. All ah know is, ever since she scared me in mid pee, my prostrate has been actin up sumthin fierce.

Them two little kitties are growin up real fast, en our older cat name uv Brother don't like it one dang bit. They still play pretty hard, en the other day they got carried away en knocked Jan's crystal candy dish off the table en broke it. Boy howdy, ah thought Donald Duck was in the house, the way Jan was a squawkin at them terrorists (that's what she calls them two kitties when she gets mad at them.)

Oh yeah, Bob en Jan en Walker en Martha are plannin to put me en Brother en the terrorists in a dog en cat prison while they go down to Florida to see Granny en J.B. en Lois en ever-buddy. Now them cats can speak fer theirselves, but ah want to go too! But Bob says no, ah got fleas en not only that, my breath stinks en he don't want to be cooped up in our car with my bad breath fer twelve er thirteen hours, en not only that, they ain't enough room in the car fer all uv us, en besides, he don't want me carryin my fleas into Granny's er J.B. en Lois' houses.

Well, that's about it — my back iz gettin tired sittin up here a peckin away on this here keybored. So tell everbuddy hi fer me, en y'all take it easy now you hear?

Luv,

Sherlock

HOW BOUT THEM MISSISSIPPI STATE UNIVERSITY BASSET HOUNDS!

Dear Mr. en Miz. Howell,

We ain't never met, but ah know U know all about me on a count uv Bob tells on me whenever he sends you a Chrismas card there in Tennessee ever year. En I read yore Christmas cards, en Bob has told me uh hole bunch of stories of when you all were neighbors in Landers' Mobil Home Park when you were all goin' to Mississippi State University there in Starkville.

Bob iz lookin over mah shoulder, en he sed it would be OK if ah called you Doug en Pam. So do U still call Steven by the nickname uv Rufus on a count uv his red hair? Bob doesn't have uh nickname fer me, but he does have a nickname fer when ah do mah bidness outside. He calls it a Lawrence Welk. U know, on the Lawrence Welk TV show when he starts off a song he always says "A one, and a two..." Sew if'n ah do a number one *en* a number two outside, he tells Jan ah done uh Lawrence Welk.

Speakin uv names, it really bothers Bob that Mississippi State University iz called the Bulldogs on a count uv University of Georgia iz called the Bulldogs en that purty much ruins a bulldog's reputation everwhere. Ah know, ah know, Bob got his undergraduate degree at Florida, en he iz uh dye hard Gator fan; sew he might be comin down kinda hard on this, but ennyhow don't U think Mississippi State would be a hole lot better off bein the MSU Basset Hounds? Sounds good, don't it! Tell ever-buddy U know en git em to start a rite-in campaign.

OK. New subject: Ah figger ah would go to a expert on

this situation, en Bob says you know all about animal science en agerculcher en plants en all like that, Doug. Sew hear goes:

1. Will dog wee-wee actshully kill Jan's favorite azalea bushes? Ah M lookin fer U to come down on the side of "NO" on this one. It shore would help me a lot.

2. Say a dog, oh maybe a basset hound, was to drop his right shoulder into a ripe cow plopper and roll on over on his back on said cowplopper. Would this evenchully cause his right leg to grow twice as long as his left leg, like Bob says? I'm purty worried about this one on a count of old habits die hard; sew I hope U rite me back soon on that answer.

Yore frend furever,

Sherlock

AH JUST SORT UV LOST TRACK UV TIME

Deer Granny,

How R U? Ah M fyne.

Bob iz teachin me how to plan my time better. It all started the other day when ah come back from a long, meanderin walk on my own. Bob said, "Where have you been? Ah was worried sick! You didn't leave a note where you were goin! Ah thought you might have gotten run over er sumbody had kidnapped you er sumthin!"

I told him the truth. Ah said, "Ah dunno. Ah just sort uv lost track uv the time."

Bob said, "Sherlock, you got to plan your time better. Let me show you. Before Jan went shoppin she asked me to do the laundry. Ah will show you how ah put a plan together en work the plan. You can watch me en keep track uv my progress."

Planned Activity by Bob
Estimated Time
- Put dirty clothes in washin machine.
  1 minute
- Put in soap.
  0 minutes, 10 seconds
- Set the dial.
  0 minutes, 5 seconds
- Push the start button.
  0 minutes, 1 second
- When done, put clothes in dryer.
  0 minutes, 1 minute

- Turn dial to the right settin.
  0 minutes, 5 seconds
- Push the start button.
  0 minutes, 1 second
- When dryer dings, take clothes out.
  1 minute
- Put on dinin room table.
  1 minute
- Fold en put away.
  10 minutes

Total estimated time
13 minutes, 23 seconds

Actual Activities Watched by Me
Actual Time

- Gather up clothes — too much fer one load.
  3 minutes.
- Separate out whites from colors.
  4 minutes.
- Look under beds, etc. fer unmatched dirty socks.
  10 minutes.
- Open washin machine lid.
  0 minutes, 1 second.
- Notice the previously washed load uv clothes still in washin machine.
  0 minutes, 1 second.
- Take previously washed load uv clothes out uv the washin machine.
  1 minute.
- Open dryer door en notice a load uv previously dried clothes still in dryer.
  0 minutes, 2 seconds.

- Put wet load uv clothes down, take dried clothes out uv dryer to the dinin room table.
  2 minutes
- Notice they iz no room on dinin room table because it iz full uv clothes dried earlier by Jan.
  0 minutes, 1 second.
- Put load uv clothes he iz holdin on livin room sofa
  0 minutes, 30 seconds.
- Fold clothes on dinin room table.
  15 minutes
- Bonus! Found 3 matchin socks that go with the dirty socks to be washed.
  0 minutes, 1 second.
- Put folded clothes away.
  10 minutes
- Take clothes off uv sofa en put on dinin room table.
  0 minutes, 30 seconds.
- Go put the wet washed clothes in the dryer
  1 minute
- Set the dryer dial, push start button.
  0 minutes, 15 seconds.
- Bob gets to finally put his first load uv dirty clothes into washer.
  1 minute.
- Realize didn't put softener sheet in dryer. Stop it, put softener sheet in. Restart.
  0 minutes, 20 seconds.
- Put soap in washer. Ran out uv soap. Only had about 1/2 amount needed. Use liquid dish soap to make up difference.
  1 minute.

- Set washin machine dial. Push start button.
  0 minutes, 10 seconds.
- Drive to grocery store. Get laundry detergent. Drive home.
  50 minutes.
- Suds all over the laundry room floor from the liquid dish soap. Clean up the mess.
  55 minutes.
- Take clothes out uv dryer (remember them?) en put on dinin room table.
  I minute, 40 seconds.
- Take Bob's first batch uv clothes out uv washer en put them in dryer, set dial, start it.
  2 minutes.
- Out uv softener sheets. Think about it. Talk to God and Jesus briefly.
  Decide to not go to grocery store to git more. Dry without them.
  0 minute, 21 seconds.
- Put Bob's second batch uv clothes in washer.
  I minute.
- Set dial. Start
  0 minutes, 12 seconds (Ha! He iz gettin faster!)
- Fold clothes on dinin room table
  20 minutes
- Put clothes away.
  15 minutes.
- Cruise channels on the TV while dryer iz still runnin
  15 minutes.
- Take Bob's first batch uv clothes out uv dryer en put on dinin room table.

Count zero. Don't sweat the small stuff.

- Put Bob's second batch uv clothes in dryer, set dial, start it.
  Ditto.
- Fold clothes on dinin room table
  20 minutes
- Put clothes away.
  15 minutes.
- Cruise channels on the TV while dryer iz still runnin.
  15 minutes.
- Open dryer door. Notice clothes smell dirty. Realize didn't put detergent into the second load uv wash.
  30 seconds.
- Put dried, unwashed clothes back in washer.
  1 minute.
- Put in laundry detergent. Set dial. Start.
  0 minutes, 18 seconds.
- Slam lid. Break top hinges on washin machine lid. Tape in place fer now with duck tape so washer will run.
  3 minutes.
- Go to hardware store to find replacement hinges. Don't have. Go to store where Bob bought washin machine to git replacement hinges. Don't have. They send Bob to an appliance parts store on the other side uv town. They have. Drive home. Stop at grocery store on the way en git softener sheets.
  2 hours, 12 minutes, forget the seconds from now on.
- Walk in house. Jan got home while Bob was out shoppin. Jan says to Bob "Where have you been? Ah was worried sick! You didn't leave a note where you were

goin! Ah thought you might have gotten run over er sumbody had kidnapped you er sumthin!" Bob says, "Ah dunno. Ah just sort uv lost track uv the time."
Oh, about 2 minutes.

- Jan has finished the wash, folded en put away Bob's second batch uv clothes. So Jan says, "By the way, thank U very much fer not doin the wash like ah asked you to."

Maybe uh minute?

Total actual time

Near az ah kin figger it, about 7 hours.

I asked Bob would he take me fer a walk. He sed "yes," but he just sort uv moped along; sew he wuzzunt much company. He didunt even notice thet ah wee-wee'd on Mister Wicker's mailbox post.

All fer now. Luv,

Sherlock

THE PURTIEST SONG THERE EVER WAS

Deer Steve, Julie en Stewart[12],
How R U? Ah M fine.

Bob told me thet U have adopted uh Laberdoar Retriever name uv Millie. Thet iz gratel Ah reely like Laberdoar Retrievers. They iz reel nice. It iz alsew uh good thang yore naybors iz got uh Basset Hound thet Millie can play with. Ah wish B.D., the mean yeller-hared dog down the street, wuz a Laberdoar Retriever. He is just plane meen. He iz allwayz in uh bad, bad mood en he takes it out on everbuddy, speshully me. Bob sez, "Well Sherlock, quit doo-dooin in hiz yard, en maybe thet will smooth thangs out." Sew ah guess ah will give thet uh try, but ah doubt it will help much.

Stewart, cungradulayshuns on getin yore drivin license! Ah hear U R getting uh hand-me-down minivan; sew U can carry awl uv yore rock band's insterments. Maybe U could name yore band "The Mini Rocker Van Men" er "The Minivan Doo Rahs" er something like thet. Ah'll work on it. Oh! Ah know! How about "The Minivan Maxiband?" No, no. Ennyhow, U drive careful in thet thing, now, U hear.

Steve, Bob sez U R the bestest consultant in the U.S. of A on how to develop en improve processes en manage em en awl like thet; so ah M attachin mah documentation frum Bob's seven hour project on not getting awl the clothes washed en dried en folded like Jan asked him to. Maybe U could give him uh few tips on cutting thet time down. He shore could use yore help.

Thank U fer sendin thet CD of songs U recorded, Steve. Bob

en Jan en me iz unanimous thet "I'm Slowly Getting Over You" is the purtiest song we ever did hear, en to think thet yore daddy rote it! Since it iz uh waltz, whenever they play it, Bob en Jan git up and dance, unless they iz in the car. I sort uv sway back en forth en dance around em, but not like those dogs on TV who dance with their lady partners en go all between their legs en whirl around backwards en awl like thet. Ah stay on the perimeter.

It is obvious U R uh good guitar player en singer. Bob prolly never told U thet he plays uh ukalaylee. Ah asked him why he duzzunt play uh guitar en he said four strings wuz enough fer him to deal with. Course he only plays uh few songs like "Froggy Went a Courtin" en uh few Kingston Trio songs en "Five Foot Two, Eyes uv Blue, Has Ennybuddy Seen My Gal." Thet "Five Foot Two" song iz gittin kind uv old; sew ah helped him make up sum new verses to it:

Five foot nine, eyes thet shine,

Face thet looks like Frankenstein,

Has ennybody seen my gal!

She can't neck, but what the heck,

She plays end fer Georgia Tech,

Has ennybuddy seen mah gal!

Ah wuz workin on another verse thet started out "She's purty en smart" but ah could only think uv one word thet rymed with "smart," if'n U know whut ah mean; sew ah had to give up on thet one.

Well, thatz uhbout it on this hear end. Ah hope U enjoy Millie az much az ah enjoy Bob en Jan!

Yore frend furevver,

Sherlock

DOUGHNUTS, TWO FER A NICKEL!

Deer Julie,

How R U? Ah M fine.

Now first off, tell Steve en Stewart not to git awl pouty on acuz ah didunt include them in this hear letter. It wuz awl about them in thuh last lettur.

Well, ennyhow in thet last letter ah got to thinking awl about their musical interests en thet got me to thinking about sum music fer U to teach the children at the skool where U werk.

See, when Bob wuz in thuh fifth grade in Miz King's class there at Central Elementary School in Ocala, Florida. Miz King loved to sing. Bob sed she would be right in thuh middle uv a histery lesson right after lunch, en she would say, "Well that's enuff histery learnin fer today, children. Let's sing!" En Miz King would pick uh song en Bob en awl thuh children in Miz. King's class would just sing away.

Miz Johnson was the principal, en Bob sed she didunt mind thuh singin one bit. He sed she wuz from Canada en had long reddish brown hair en wore horn-rimmed glasses en drove uh big dark green Hudson thet sort of looked like The Green Hornet's car en she wuz kind to awl thuh children.

Let's see, where wuz I? Oh, yeah, Bob's favorite song was one Miz King come up with herself. It wuz to the tune of "Turkey in the Straw" en it goes like this (Bob sez ah got to spel it out thuh way Miz King spelt it):

Oh, I went to Ocala, and I walked around the block.

And I walked into a baker's shop.

I picked two doughnuts out of the grease,
And I handed the lady a five cent piece.
She looked at the nickel, and she looked at me,
Said, "Gee this nickel's no good to me."
"There's a hole in the middle, and it's all the way through,"
Say, "Aye, there's a hole in the doughnuts too!"

Now I was thinking U could change "Ocala" to "Old Charlotte" fer three reasons:

One: "Charlotte," on acuz U live in Charlotte.

Two: It has to be when doughnuts wuz two fer uh nickel, en thet would reely be "old, old, old Charlotte," but to make thuh song come out right, U have to use just one "old." This is whut us song riters call poetic license.

Thurd reason is you can prolly git by with callin it uh histery lesson if you throw in the "old" word.

Bob sed Miz King's second favorite song was "Whispering Hope" en they wood do that one in four part harmony. She would also have the children sing "My Country Tis of Thee" en "My Bonnie Lies Over the Ocean" en "She'll be Comin Round thuh Mountain," but ah figger U dun got those covered. They used to sing "Way Down Upon the Suwannee River" uh lot too, but all U got over there iz thuh Catawba River en thuh Yadkin River, en neither one uv them sound right when U plug em in fer "Suwannee."

Well, thatz uhbout it on this end.

Yore frend ferevver,

Sherlock

MAH SEKERT SOCKER PLAYIN TIPS

Deer Charlton,

How R U? Ah M fyne.

Congradulayshuns on graduatin from high skool. Ah am reel proud uv you.

Well, here iz a reel surprise. For your graduwayshun present, ah am givin you thurty dollars. No, no, don't worry. Ah know you think ah worked real hard earnin that there money en ah shouldn't be a givin it away, but ah didn't have to work hard fer it. Ah won it off uv Walker en Martha playin this here game ah don't remember what you call it but you throw these here two dice en you win money, en ah won a whole bunch; sew ah am givin it to you. It iz in the sekert envelope en you can open it now.

Now this here money iz from uh nuther kuntry called Monopoly, but Bob says if'n you play thuh game rite, you kin git rich. Ah know you kin buy houses en hotels en pay to git out uv jail with it, so ah doan't see why you cain't buy a hole new set uv skool clothes, en uh sports kar en all yore skool books with it.

Now, ah know you are gettin along pretty good in socker, en you iz prolly goin to accept a college scholarship to play socker. Ah don't want to scare you, but college socker iz a whole lot harder to play than high skool socker; sew ah thought ah would pass along a few uv my socker tips ah learned from Bob. You prolly don't know this, but Bob was on the University uv Florida socker team. Ah bet you didn't even know socker was invented way back then.

Tip number one: Don't keep your eye on the ball. It iz very uncumfterbul, en besides you can do real damage makin eyeball contact with a socker ball. Not only that, you can see the ball better if'n your eyes iz about two er three inches away from the ball.

Tip number two: Keep your nose on one side er the other side uv the ball, but not right behind the ball — you can control it better that way. Also, this allows you to slobber on the ball better witch makes it harder fer the goalie to catch on a count uv the slobber makes it slippery.

Tip number three: The ideal control position iz when you are makin simultaneous contact with the ball with your chest, the bottom edge uv one side er your jaw en one knee then the other knee: one two, one two, one, two, en sew on.

Tip number four: Always play with your mouth open. If they ain't nothin worth bitin then growl a lot.

Tip number five: Tell the other team's goalie that you doo—doo'd sumwhere out there in front uv him a few feet, but you can't remember exactly where. Do this early in the game.

Tip number six: If'n the other team iz playin real physical, you know, with a lot uv unnecessary body contact, find a nearby cow pasture en find a ripe cow plopper. Drop your right shoulder in it en roll over on your back on top uv it. Then git back in the game. They ain't gonna crowd you no more.

Tip number seven: You may not agree on this here tip with me, but ah don't like to wear a jock strap; sew ah don't. First, it looks weird. Second it feels weird havin my unmentionables all scrunchied up, en third, everbuddy can tell when you take a quick wee—wee on the playin field on a count uv they see you pullin your jock strap out uv the way.

Well, that's about it on this here end.

Your frend forever,

Sherlock P. Blanchard

PORE OLD FEBRUARY

Deer Craig en Sandy,

How R U? Ah M fyne.

We shore did have uh good tyme visitin U back their in Alpharetta, Jawjuh, my home town.

Everbuddy likes yore new house. Ah like the bigger yard, and the house iz uh lot bigger en it iz reel purty en awl like that, but to tell U the truth, yore uther house didunt have enny steps on account uv it was uh ranch style like our old house acrost the street, en ah like not havin to climb up en down steps.

Ah M sorry ah give Kerri en Sarah sum wrong ansers on their spellin homework, espeshully on how to spell the months en thuh days uv thuh week, but there is no dang way there ough-ta be that "r" after the "b" in Febuary, en ah didunt think there wuz enny need for the furst "d" or the secund "e" in Wednes day. I told Bob, they wuz nobody in this world who pernounces the furst "d" in Wednesday, but there we were, drivin home en listenin to the radio, en on comes Paul Harvey. Dang if he did-unt pernounce that "d!" He even pernounces ever letter in the werd "vegetables." It's bad enough U gotta eat all yore vegtubles, but when he gits through sayin it, it sounds like you gotta eat twice as much!

I'm gonna start listenin to Paul Harvey ever day; sew ah kin hear him pernounce that there first "r" in February. Bob sez ah got uh long wait; since it is April already. Well, if ever month only had 28 days like—I cain't bring myself to spell it the "correct" way—Febuwary, then ah woodunt have to wait sew long.

En that got me to thankin—how come Febuwary ain't got 30 or 31 days like the rest uv thuh months. How come they pickin on Febuwary? Ah bet teachers come up with that; so they give students term papers to write en they give em uh deadline uv the end uv the month, en thuh students git cheated out uv three er four dayz uv goofin off afore they got to git bizzy en rite thet there term paper. Maybe it wuz one uv them wait watcher diet companys come up with it; sew when U git yore choklit candy on Valentine's Day, U no U cain't eat too much uv it on account uv U ain't got that many dayz left afore thuh end uv thuh month when U got to weigh in.

Craig, Bob sez U need to come up here in May en go fishin fer bluefish. Jan en Sandy could go shoppin fer collectibles en anteeks en stuff like that. Ah asked Bob iz there such uh thang az uh purplefish, en he sed "No, but there iz uh redfish, witch iz whut they call em in Florida, essept in North Carolina they call them uh red drum." That's OK ah guess, but whut we call uh speckled perch in Florida, they call em "crappie" in North Caro-lina. Bob sed, "Sherlock, ah hate to tell U this, but they call em "crappie" in Jawjuh too, but in Minnesota they call em "crop-pie." En then Bob sed, "Sherlock, thet would make uh good research project fer U to find out what all thuh different names are fer uh speckled perch. Why don't U giv me uh report on thet at the end uv thuh month." Thank goodness it ain't Febuwary, er ah'd be on uh short string! Maybe ah could send all uv thuh names to Paul Harvey to pernounce, en people could call in en vote fer the name thy liked the best. Ah woodunt place no bets on "crappie," thets fer shore.

Yore frend ferrever,

Sherlock

JAN WON'T LET ME CASH IN MY "GOOD BOY" CREDITS

Memo to: Kady M. and Trisha J.[13]
Frum: Sherlock P. Blanchard
Subject: Legal Loopholes fer "Good Boy" Credits
Dear Kady en Trisha,

Ah M ritin to U on a count uv U R both in the legal perfession en deel with criminals. See, ah know that criminals in prison git rewarded fer good behavior lak git out uv jail early en stuff lak thet. Now the criminal iz in prison fer bad behavior en the good behavior comes after.

But ah wont to turn thet around. Whut ah M tryin to sell Jan on iz gettin credit fer good behavior afore ah do uh bad thing. That way ah doan't git punished when thuh bad thang comes along, doan't U see. Lak the other day Jan called me to come to her en she sed "Good boy." Then ah held still while she hooked up the leash en she sed "Good boy." Then ah walked along aside her without pullin on the leash en she sed "Good boy!" Sew ah figgered ah had three "Good boys" saved up rat there. Well, uh littul later thet day ah got in thuh garbage en spread it around in the kitchen—U know, the lettuce en coffee grounds en stuff lak that ah ain't gonna eat. Ah figgered not eaten the bad stuff was worth another "Good boy;" sew thet made four uv em, but noooooo! Jan come in en saw that mess en U kin fergit about awl uh them "Good boys." She got after me lak ah ain't dun uh "Good boy" thang in mah hole life!

Sew if U kin dig up sum legal mumbo jumbo ipso facto

sumthin er uther about "Good boy" credit that wood hep my case with Jan pleeze let me know. Bob sed ask U sumthin uhbout haybeus corpses, but ah doan't wont Jan hearin nuthin uhbout no corpses cuz she dun sed she could kill me fer whut ah did.

Now Trisha, ah M sendin your brother Gerry uh copy uv this hear memo own a count uv he knows all about sports players, includin thuh trubbel they git into. Now ah know when Bear Bryant was coachin Alabama he wuz uh hole lot lak Jan. It didn't matter how many "Good boy" credits Joe Namath had, if he broke uh team rule, he got punished jest lak ever buddy else on the team. But nowadays they iz this here coach, ah ain't gonna name him, but his team's arch enemy iz the Florida Gators (this ought to keep hiz identify sekert cause that could be ten er twelve different teams). Course if ah told U hiz team ain't in the SEC that might narrow it down too much; so ah woant say that. Ennyhow this here coach, when won uv hiz star players does sumthin bad, thuh coach doan't punish them near az much az his second string players. Ah figger Gerry could help me make thuh case thet by Jan not punishin me lak thet coach, it motivates me to be a really good boy. Thuh Florida Gators iz mine en Bob's favorite team, but their coach ain't no help in my case on acuz he punishes bad behavior no matter who does it.

Kady, ah M also sendin uh copy uv this hear memo to yore brother, name uv Chuck Hayes. U hav told me Chuck enjoys mah letters, en he could help me make the case thet if Jan punished me all the time, thet iz awl ah wood rite uhbout en thet woodunt be uh hole lot uv fun to read about.

Sew, thankew all fer yore help. Ah M givin U credit fer doin sum good things fer helpin me; sew if you ever git a tikkit fer speedin er spittin on thuh sidewalk er sumthin er other, ah wil testify on yore behaff uhbout your good deeds, doan't ewe see, en U will git off scot free.

DEER AINT PEGGY

Yore frend forever,

Sherlock P. Blanchard

THEY IZ MOAR THEN WON WAYE TWO SPEL ENNY WERD

Note: Sherlock lays it on pretty thick here to help Bob and Jan's nephew. You probably ought to read this letter aloud to hear what it is saying. Also, to spare the glossary an undue burden, Sherlock's letter is translated in its entirety immediately following his letter.—Bob

Deer Spencer,

Hear iz uh kopy uv thuh letter ah sent two yore fifth grade teacher.

Ah hope this heps, but don't hold yore breth on acuz she prolly ain't gonna buy it, but we gotta keep tryin two win her over.

Yore frend furever,

Sherlock

Deer Miz Utterback,

We aint ben innerduced yet, butt furst off, ah rite in thuh modurn fonetical waye; sew if'n ewe hav trubbel reedin this hear lettur, jest reed it ouwt loud, souwndin thuh werdz foneticly, en U wil unnerstand it reel eezy.

Ah M ritin two U own beehaff uv my neffew Spencer hoo iz in yore klass. Ackshully, hee aint mah neffew. Sea, ah M uh Basset Hound hoo livz wif Bob en Jan. Jan iz thuh sistur uv Spencer's Muther, nayme uv Charleen; sew teknicly ah M Spencer's cuzzin, butt ah kawl hem mah neffew own uh kount uv ah M oaldur then hem.

Wel, ennyhow, Spencer rote two me en tole me how U wuz givvin hem uh lot uv trubbel uhbout hiz nu waye uv spellin. Sea, Spencer akwired hiz flare fer spellin frum reedin thuh letturz ah rote two hem en hiz famly. Now Spencer iz uh reel goed speller inn whut U kawl "thuh propper waye two spel"—jest chek wif hiz teeechurs frum yeers passed, but me en Spencer iz ouwt their own thuh frunt lynes uv uh revulooshin in how two spel en rite. Nouw U gott two be flexubul abouwt this hear spellin, Miz Udderback. Thuh werld iz passin ewe bye. Nouw, thuh waye ah figger hit, thuh hole idee beehind spellin iz thet U R capturin thuh spoaken werd wif uh bunche uv letturz whut souwndz lak thuh werd. Wel, thet iz ezzackly whut ah M doin, butt ah doan't wurry uhbouwt thuh won en onlyest waye two ezzackly spel uh werd. Our won rool fer spellin iz: if'n it sounz rite it iz spelt rite. Jest thank uv thuh producktivvity thet riters en novullists en noozepayper edditerz en awl lak thet wil gane. Thay woan't be waystin any tyme lookin upp houw two spell thuh werdz. This wil free thim upp two jest goe fer it en rite there idees douwn en git it dun. Ah figger this hear modurn fonettikul waye uv spellin wil prolly inkreese ritin producktivvity bye thutty er fortee pursent minnowmum.

Now, U may argew thet it taykes loanger two reed. Wel, everbuddy nose it taykes uh hole lot loanger two rite sumthin then it duz two reed it. Sew we iz speedin up thuh long thang (ritin) uh hole lot en slowin down thuh fast thang (reedin) uh littul bit. Asidez, peepul R allus reedin two fast ennyhow. Haff thuh tyme they doan't evun reed thuh stuff en jest skim ovur it. Peepul git hi blood preshure en ulserz reedin sew fast. Wif this hear modurn foneticul waye uv spelin, peepul wil slow down thuh pace uv reedin, tayke it eezy, lower there blood preshure, en reduse thuh nummer uv ulsers in there stummik. Sew this hear methud wil improove everbuddy's helth.

They iz uh hole lot uhbout thuh Anglish way uv spellin thet iz purty dumb. Fer ezzampul:

Whar in thuh werld did thet their *ph* fer uh *f* souwnd kum frum? Woodn't it be uh hole lot simpuler en les kunfusin two spel them werdz wif uh *f?* Lak *Filadelfia, fillosofer, Fillips Petroleum, fonetic,* etc.

En sumtymez *gh* iz pernounsed lak uh *f,* fur ezzampul *enough,* en bye thuh waye thatt their *o* weren't needed. Sew thuh modurn fonetticul spellin wood be: *enuf.* En thuh Anglish mayd it evun moar komplikated, on acuz sumtimez *gh* iz pernounsed lak a *w!* Thets rite! A dang *W!* Fur ezzampul: *though.* En hear we goe uhgin, thuh *u* aint evun neaded. Mah impruved spellin wood bee: *tho.*

Bob sez if'n you R reely seereous uhbout teechin them childrun propper Ainglish lak it iz spoke in Aingland, ewe wood haff two teech thuh childrun two say *bloody,* lak hand in yore bloody hoamwerk, en pleeze pass thuh bloody pees en karrots. Now, how wood ewe lak two hav thet own yore handz? U no Miz Uderbak, us Umerrikuns gott our endeependunse from Ainglund, lessee nouw, how minny yeerz? Putt douwn 3, karry yore 2, thutty dayz hav Septimbur, April, 28, won putater, too putater, three putater fore. No, no, thet aint rite. Wel we dun ben indupendent uh hole long tyme, en we evun gott sum indupenunce wif our langwidge. Ah meen they iz werdz we uze thet thuh Ainglish doan't hav. Werdz lak: *homerun, touchdown, sweet ice tea, crappie (thuh fish), keepin on, yeeeeehaaaaa, redneck, trunk (uv uh kar. They kawl it uh boot), hood (they kawl it uh bonnet),* etc. etc. Sew we hav modurnized thet their olde Ainglish. It ownly standz two reezin thet we shood modurnize thuh waye we spel. En we awt two kawl it Uhmerrikun, knot Ainglish. It iz Our paytreeotic dooty two goe ovur to this hear modurn foneticul waye uv spellin lak me en Spencer.

Wy it shood be uh onner, Miz Uderbak, fer U two be uhlowwin Spencer two leed thuh waye in this prugressiv, perduktiv, helth improovin, paytreeottik methud uv spellin. Yep, win me en Spencer git uh Presidenchul Meddle uv Onner won uh theze dayz, ah M gonna sind ewe uh Grayhouwnd Buss Tikkit two kum two Washinton Dee Cee en sit own thuh frunt row, en win thuh Prezident, wy win she puts thet there mettle own Spencer, him en me wil turn two thuh awdeeunce en ask ewe two stand up en we wil saye, "Wee ow it awl two Miz Uderbak."

Sew thenk ewe, Miz Uderbak, en God Bless Umerrikuh.

Yore frend furevvur,

Sherlock P. Blanchard

Translation of the letter: They Iz Moar Then Won Waye
Two Spel Enny Werd

There Is More than One Way To Spell Any Word

Dear Miss Utterback,

We haven't been introduced yet, but first off, I write in the modern phonetical way; so if you have trouble reading this here letter, just read it out loud, sounding the words phonetically, and you will understand it real easy.

I am writing to you on behalf of my nephew Spencer who is in your class. Actually, he ain't my nephew. See, I am a Basset Hound who lives with Bob and Jan. Jan is the sister of Spencer's Mother, name of Charleen; so technically I am Spencer's cousin, but I call him my nephew on account of I am older than him.

Well, anyhow, Spencer wrote to me and told me how you were giving him a lot of trouble about his spelling. See, Spencer acquired his flair for spelling from reading the letters I wrote to him and his family. Now Spencer is a real good speller un what you call "the proper way to spell"—just check with his teachers from years past, but me and Spencer is out there on the front lines of a revolution in how to spell and write. Now you got to be flexible about this here spelling, Miss Utterback. The world is passing you by. Now, the way I figure it, the whole idea behind spelling is that you are capturing the spoken word with a bunch of letters what sounds like the word. Well, that is exactly what I am doing, but I don't worry about the one and only way to exactly spell a word. Our one rule for spelling is: If it sounds right it is spelled right.

Just think of the productivity that writers and novelists and newspaper editors and all like that will gain. They won't be wasting any time looking up how to spell the words. This will free them up to just go for it and write their ideas down and get it done. I figure this here modern phonetical way of spelling will probably increase writing productivity by thirty of forty percent minimum.

Now, you may argue that it takes longer to read. Well, everybody knows it takes a whole lot longer to write something than it does to read it. So we are speeding up the long thing (writing) a whole lot and slowing down the fast thing (reading) a little bit. Besides, people are always reading too fast anyhow. Half the time they don't even read the stuff and just skim over it. People get high blood pressure and ulcers reading so fast. With this here modern phonetical way of spelling, people will slow down the pace of reading, take it easy, lower their blood pressure, and reduce the number of ulcers in their stomach. So this here method will improve everybody's health.

There is a whole lot about the English way of spelling that is pretty dumb. For example:

Where in the world did that there *ph* for an *f* sound come from? Wouldn't it be a whole lot simpler and less confusing to spell them words with an *f*? Like *Filadelfia, fillosofer, Fillips Petroleum, fonetic,* etc.

And sometimes *gh* is pronounced like an *f,* for example: *enough,* (and by the way that there *o* wasn't needed). So the modern phonetical spelling would be: *enuf.*

And the English made it even more complicated because sometimes *gh* is pronounce like a *w!* That's right! A dang *W!* For example: *though.* And here we go again, the *u* ain't even needed. My improved spelling would be: *thow.*

Bob says if you are really serious about teaching them children proper English like it is spoken in England, you would have to teach the children to say *bloody,* like hand in your bloody homework, and pass the bloody peas. Now, how would you like to have that on your hands? You know Miss Utterback, we Americans got our independence from England, let's see now, how many years? Put down 3, carry your 2, thirty days have September, April, 28, one potato, two potato, three potato four. No, no, that ain't right. Well we done been independent a whole long time, and we even got some independence with our language. I mean there are words we use that the English don't have. Words like *homerun, touchdown, sweet ice tea, crappie (the fish) keeping on, yeeeeehuuuuu, redneck, trunk (of a car— they call it a boot), hood (they call it a bonnet)*, etc. So we have modernized that there olde English. It only stands to reason that we should modernize the way we spell. And we ought to call it American, not English. It is our patriotic duty to go over to this here modern phonetical way of spelling like me and Spencer.

Why it should be an honor, Miss Utterback, for you to be allowing Spencer to lead the way in this progressive, productive, health-improving, patriotic method of spelling. Yep, when me and Spencer get a Presidential Medal of Honor one of these days, I am going to send you a Greyhound bus ticket to come to Washington D.C. and sit on the front row, and when the President, why when she puts that there medal on Spencer, him and me will turn to the audience and ask you to stand up and we will say, "We owe it all to Miss Utterback."

So thank you, Miss Utterback, and God Bless America.

Your friend forever,

Sherlock P. Blanchard

MY FAMILY HISTORY BY SHERLOCK PERRY BLANCHARD

Deer Unkel Joe en Aint Bobbye Nann,

How R U? Ah M fyne. We got your letter about providin our family history. Well, you know Bob en Jan. It will take them forever to git theirs done. But ah done mine already en here it is.

Ah was born at an early age on a warm day in November. Ah was born in a basement uv a house what belonged to a banker en his wife who was a graduate uv Agnes Scott College fer Women — the wife, not the banker. The house was in North Atlanta about a mile from the governor's mansion. Even though the governor was a neighbor, we never was innerduced; although ah wee-wee'd on his fence posts regular.

Ennyhow, the first thang ah remember was my mother grabbin me on the top uv my head en pullin me out uv her birth canal cause ah was stuck, me bein the biggest uv six children. Good thang ah was the last, otherwise sum uv my brothers en sisters would have real scrunchy-up short noses. Where was I? Oh yeah, well she bit into the top uv my head en pulled me right out, en in doin sew pulled a small spot uv fur off uv the top uv my head witch iz bald to this day witch iz why ah git a sunburn real easy. Mama also actually bit into my skull en caused a bony knot on my head en you know the rest uv that story. Other words, Granny knows what she iz talkin about when she calls me knot head.

Well, ah got three brothers en two sisters: Bullet, Slew Foot, Zippy, Elvira, en Marilyn. Bullet was a great hunter en hunted rabbits, possums, en Jackunese beetles until one day while trackin a rabbit he was bit by a six foot long rattle snake right on his ear en one fang went right through his ear near the bottom edge, en luckily the poison squirted out on the other side, but ever since old Bullet don't hunt no more en he has put a gold ear ring in that there fang hole in his ear en he talks with a lithp.

Slew foot become the official mascot uv the Hickory Flats Junior High School fightin Tigers on a count uv they couldn't find no tigers en besides, Slew Foot charges a cheaper rate. Zippy sells repossessed mobile homes in Pothole Corners, Georgia. Zippy has a bad habit uv eatin prunes en bran cereal ever night before he goes to bed. Then in the mornin he goes along the town's only joggin trail doin number twos en number ones all over the place witch iz where the expression "zippy-tee-doo-dah" comes from.

Elvira took a baby sitter job near our original home. She got on the Wheel uv Fortune TV program with Vanna White a couple uv years ago. She won big by just howlin out them vowels, en iz now retired from baby sittin. Marilyn married a Afghan Hound en they proceeded to have twelve uv the ugliest kids you ever did see. She also converted to her husband's religion en now won't eat no pork er Alpo. They took off fer Paducah, Kentucky a couple years ago, en ah ain't seen nor heard from her since.

Me uv course, ah become a writer en philosopher, givin up on my original dream uv bein a TV repair man. Ah signed up fer this hear "Learn To Be A TV Repair Man In Ten Easy Lessons At Home" through a correspondence course. But then half way down the third page uv Chapter One, it said "Grasp the reiterater between your thumb en forefinger en gently pull over en out." Well, since ah ain't got no thumb er forefinger, ah grabbed that there sucker with my teeth, en it shocked the zippy-tee-doo-dah out uv me. Well, ah give up TV repair right there in the spot. Ah still have a sekert ambition to be a hare dresser. Get it? Hare dresser. Hare. Rabbit. Haw! Haw! Haw!

CHILDHOOD: Well, mine was pretty normal. Ah got my share uv whippins, ah picked my nose regular, ah didn't brush my teeth after ever meal, ah could chew spinach without ever swallowin it, ah could throw a pretty good temper tantrum, ah could chase the ice cream truck with the best uv them, en ah used Clearasil pimple sucker medicine — the pimples bein caused by eatin too many cookies.

THEN when ah was two years old, ah started chewin tobacco en cussin on a regular basis; although ah had pretty good grades in school. Ah smoked a cigar once. Make that twice — my first en my last time.

Durin high school ah won letters fer javelin catchin in track, en in swimmin ah won a letter fer the modified breast stroke — otherwise known as dog paddlin. Ah went out fer center on the football team, but by the time ah got the ball back between my hind legs, everbuddy would have already jumped off sides. Besides, ah didn't like where that quarter back put his hands. Also, the defensive position acrost from the center iz called the nose guard, witch ah took personal.

Oh yeah, ah quit chewin tobacco when ah went out fer swimmin — you spit that stuff out in the pool en everbuddy knows you ain't chewin bubble gum. Ah still cuss a little—U know, like "heck" en "dang.". Sum habits die hard.

FAMOUS ANCESTORS: My mother was a grand champion sumthin er other en she could sing real good, especially when there was a full moon er a empty food dish. Ah never knew my daddy, but Mama said he was a country gentleman uv fine breedin en was real regal. His name was Goat Breath. Her name was Clara.

One uv my great, great, great uncles chased a rabbit through the back yard uv Robert E. Lee's second cousin once, en my daddy's mother-in-law from his second marriage was distantly related to Lassie.

I ain't married, an sew ah don't have no kids.

THE END

Sherlock P. Blanchard

THEY IZ A WHOLE LOT UV PINEAPPLE TREES IN MIAMI

Deer Leigh,

How R U? Ah M fyne.

Ah figgered ah would rite to U en give U sum advice about makin frends en all like that your first few days at college. Since you are goin to college in the mountins at Western Carolina, they ain't goin to be many people who know much about where you come from down there in Miami, Florida. Everbuddy in North Carolina iz real interestin en nice, but you will have to be careful not to sound uppity when they ask you questions about Miami.

So, here are the kinds uv questions you will prolly get. Ah have wrote up sum good answers fer you that iz shore to win U uh hole bunch uv new frends.

Question: Where you frum? Answer: "Miami."

Question: Well, where iz your ami? Answer: "That's a very good question. Would you excuse me, ah gotta go trim my toenails." (Leave quick. This student ain't gonna make it through the first semester.)

Question: Do you know David Caruso who iz on that TV program? Answer: "We ain't been innerduced, but ah saw him drivin down Main Street (don't say Biscayne Boulevard er they'll think you iz uppity), en you look a lot like him right around the eyebrows."

Note: To be a good conversationalist, you can't just say "yes" er "no." You got to add a little extra, like this next one:

Question: Have you ever eaten a coconut? Answer: "Yes. The inside part iz tastier than the outside part en ain't sew chewy."

Note: Sumtimes you got to explain thangs in terms your new frends can relate to. For example:

Question: What's a mango? Answer: "Well, it iz just like a watermelon, except fer the seeds — it only has one witch iz real hard to spit out if'n you git it in your mouth. En a mango ain't green on the outside, it iz red en yellow en sum green, en the part you eat iz yellow–gold like, en it's a whole lot smaller than a watermelon en it tastes a whole lot different, but other than that, it iz exactly like a watermelon — except a mango grows on a tree."

Note: Sumtimes you gotta lie, because the truth don't sound right. In this case, if'n you tell the truth they iz gonna laugh at you en you won't have no credibility. Here iz a example:

Question: Is they many pineapple trees in Miami? Answer: "Yes. They all over the place."

Question: Is they a lot uv drugs in Miami? Answer: "Yes. Walgreens has purty good prices, but ah buy my suntan lotion at Rexall."

Here iz uh hole bunch uv beach questions:

Question: Did you go to the beach ever day? Answer: "I went ever chance ah could when ah wasn't busy sloppin the hogs er pickin pineapples er haulin watermelons.

Question: Does everbuddy wear bikinis in Miami? Answer: "No. My Daddy's name iz Buddy, en he don't wear no bikini."

Question: Do you wear a bikini? Answer: "Yes. Except when ah am sloppin the hogs, pickin pineapples er eatin a mango."

Question: Ain't you afraid uv sharks? Answer: "No. They iz mostly man eaters, en ah am a girl. They iz a such a thang as a nurse shark; sew ah don't wear no nurses uniform when ah go swimmin."

Question: How far iz Miami from here? Answer: "Well, it iz 836 miles from Miami to here, but it iz only 810 miles from here to Miami on acuz it iz mostly down hill, en you can drive faster."

Question: Is they a lot uv Cubans in Miami? Answer: "Si. Mucho Buncho."

Question: Do you speak Spanish? Answer: "Jawol. Ik sprekken klein Spanish."

Hear iz sum wildlife questions:

Question: Is they a whole bunch uv alligators en crocodiles in Miami? Answer: "Yes. En it iz a real problem, on acuz most uv them iz unemployed en illiterate, en they just lie around in the parks near the ponds."

Question: What's the Everglades like? Answer: "It iz like the mountains around here, except flatter en wetter en it ain't hardly got no trees, en they ain't as much snow."

OK, next ah have a little advice about bein on a date with a boy that ain't mindin his manners, if'n you know what ah mean.

If a feller iz tryin to talk you into sumthin you don't want to do, then you say, "Listen here, my Mama sewed a quarter inside my bra, en if'n you can help me git it out uv there, we can call her en you can ask her if'n it iz all right to do what you want to do."

Now, if'n that don't work, you say, "Looka here! My Uncle Bob has this here killer attack basset hound, en if'n you don't quit, I'm gonna sick him on you. He's been trained to go fer the throat if you are less than four feet tall. Otherwise he goes fer a unmentionable part uv your body, en with his jaws uv steel, the next time you wee wee, you will think you got a lawn sprinkler hooked up down there!"

Well, that's about it on this hear end.

Oh yeah. Bob en Jan en Walker en Martha say howdy. Walker wants to know what kind uv car your roommate has. Martha wants to know if you have met any interestin en nice boys. En Bob wants to know if you have seen any trout in the stream runnin through the campus. Jan wants to know if you are eatin right en gettin enough sleep.

Yore frend forever,
Sherlock

IT DON'T MATTER WHETHER IT IZ A VERB
ER A ADJECTIVE: BITIN CATS IZ DANGEROUS!

Deer Herbert,

How R U? Am M fyne.

Aint Etta Mae[14] was tellin me how you don't see why usin the English language correctly iz sew important ennyhow. Aint Etta Mae said since my letters might have given you the idea that it iz OK to be completely flexible in your use uv language that ah should write to you en help her answer the question: Why iz it important to use the English language correctly?

Well, here goes.

Sometimes the way thangs iz said er written gives you twice as much to worry about. Bitin cats iz dangerous. Does this mean cats that bite are dangerous, er does it mean it iz dangerous fer me to bite cats?

You got to be able to say what you mean. For example, if'n you go into a restaurant en say to the waitress, "I want breakfast just like it iz cooked on a Boy Scout campin trip." you will prol-ly be disappointed. What you should have said is, "I want burnt toast, cold coffee, soupy grits, flies on my fried eggs, en sum spilled milk." Another example: Suppose you tell your parents you hope they give you a safe, reliable vehicle to drive to school. It ain't their fault if they git you a five-year-old small-sized Ford er Shivverlay when what you really wanted was a used highway patrol car with two shotguns, bullet-proof glass, good tires en a full tank uv gas. Course since you ain't old enough to drive yet, you shouldn't have gotten either one; sew be glad fer what you do get.

Sometimes the way you say sumthin makes people believe one thang when you really mean sumthin else: Five years ago ah used Ipana Toothpaste. Since then ah have used no other. Now you prolly think the guy who said that uses nothin but Ipana Toothpaste. The truth iz he ain't brushed his teeth in five years. Salesmen use this here technique en figure it's your problem if you don't interpret it "correctly." For example a used-car salesman might say, "Yes sir, this iz a fine car. Ah don't know a thang that iz wrong with it." Technically he iz tellin the truth in his second sentence; because he doesn't know anythang about the car. Bob always tells a salesman like that, "I hope you git everthang you deserve." (witch, if he interprets it correctly, iz nothin).

Sometimes leavin a word out can cost you twice as much. fer example: Your bicycle brakes don't work because the re-iterator er the thangamabob was broken. Does this mean either the re-iterator er the thangamabob was broken, er does it mean the re-iterator otherwise known as the thangamabob was broken? Now, if'n this iz what the bicycle shop tells you, you better watch out he ain't chargin you fer two parts instead uv just one.

You can be more polite if you are more adept at language. For example: Instead uv sayin, "Look! Who are them rednecks?" you can say, "Behold! What manner uv men are they with the crimson anatomy twixt head en shoulders?"

And sumtimes just a little rearrangin uv the order uv the words will make a big difference. For example, suppose your brother Leon iz workin at Felton Hookerton's garage fer the summer. Mr. Lawtell drops his car off to be fixed, en he leaves the garage a note: "Well ah don't know, but it seems to me the rear engine bracket iz loose. Fix it!" So, Leon comes in to work, reads the note, en pulls the files on Mr. Lawtell. The files say, "This here man iz a know-it-all, en iz real hard to git along with.

What ever he tells you to do, you do it, even though it iz prolly the wrong thang to do on acuz he usually don't know what he iz talkin about." The rear engine bracket iz loose. So Leon opens up the trunk en they ain't no rear engine. They iz just a engine in the front. Leon iz done got a dilemma uv major proportions en figures he iz about to lose his job. He iz only able to eat three uv his four baloney sandwiches at lunch, en can't drink but half uv his CoCola he iz sew upset. See, if Mr. Lawtell had just wrote, " The bracket at the rear uv the engine iz loose." everthang would have been fine. Except it was prolly the engine that's loooe en the bracket iz fine.

Now, they iz one modern grammar rule ah don't go along with — leavin that there comma out before the and in a string uv words. For example: Herbert's brothers are Leon, Billy Bob en Jessie. See how they ain't no comma before the en Jessie? Well what about this? The colors uv dresses Aint Etta Mae has iz red, blue, black en white. Now we know she has red dresses. En we know she has blue dresses. But now the trubble starts. Does she have a dress that iz black en white, er does she have a dress that iz black en a dress that iz white? Puttin a comma before the en would have cleared that right up. Course they missed the fact that Aint Etta Mae has a real pretty green dress en a nice yellow dress too. Ennyhow, they iz divided opinion about this comma bidness. Jan says, "When in doubt, leave it out." Me en Bob come down on the side uv "When in doubt, don't leave it out." Unfortunately your English teacher will side with Jan on this one; sew maybe you got to go along to git along.

Just one little word can make a big difference in the decisions you make in life. For example, suppose you want to go to the picture show before you clean your room en your Mama says, "If'n you go to the picture show before you clean your room, your daddy **and** I will whoop you." You would prolly clean your room first. But if'n your Mama says, "If'n you go to the picture show before you clean your room, your daddy or I will whoop you," you would prolly go to the show first, since you are only goin to git half the lickin you deserve. Well, actually if'n your daddy does it you'll git 3/4 the lickin you deserve. If your Mama does it you'll git 1/4 the lickin you deserve. So if'n ah was you, ah would quit workin on my room right now en run on down to an early picture show that gets out long before your Daddy gets home from work. That way you'll take your licks from your Mama.

And don't do no double negatives like ah do. When you say "I ain't got no pocket knife on me." Ah know ezzackly what you mean. But them teachers figure if you ain't got no, then what do you have, en you prolly got that there knife in a sekert pocket sumwhere. They'll prolly strip search you afore it's over with.

Well Herbert, that's about it on this end. Ah don't think you are goin to be able to negotiate your way out uv doin better in English class; sew ah guess you're just goin to have to learn it well. Just keep in mind they iz one thang both you en your teachers agree on: The three best thangs about school iz June, July en August, en that ain't too far off.

Your frend forever,

Sherlock

AH BEEN THINKIN ABOUT GROWIN A MUSTACHE

Deer Leigh,

How R U? Ah M fyne.

Guess whut? No, you ain't never goin to guess, sew ah will tell you. You remember about three er four years ago when Bob en Jan en Walker en Martha was in Belgium en Bob come to the U.S. uv A. on a bidness trip en he went to see Uncle Hugh en Aint Peggy in Texas en then he went to Miami to see you-all en he had this here British fellow with him, his name was Richard Swaine, en he was real interestin en nice? Well, old Richard come to see us last weekend! He had been to Singapore en Tokyo on a bidness trip en he stopped by on his way back to England. Well, he come at a good time cause last weekend was the North Carolina State Fair.

And speakin uv the fair, Bob en Jan say you ought to bring a frend er two over next year to see the fair, en stay over a couple nights with us.

Well, ah been thinkin about growin a mustache. If ah knew what color it would be ah would. Bob says if ah tried to grow a mustache it would prolly come out in the wrong place, like on my shoulder er sumthin.

Walker iz doin pretty good. He iz spendin all uv his hard-earned money on his car. He got sum dual exhausts put on Stang (that's what he calls his Mustang — Stang). Ennyhow, they iz made uv this here space age, withstands forty seven hundred degrees uv heat type uv stuff with these real good soundin Hollywood mufflers. En last week he installed a air horn — actually three air horns witch play a bugle charge er sumthin er other. First time he cut them thangs loose ah dang near jumped out uv my skin. Don't tell nobody, but ah also peed a little bit too, but that's okay, cause ah was outside at the time. Well, ennyhow, Bob says he never spent no money on his car when he was Walker's age, cause he spent all his money on girls. Jan says, "Yeah, that's what you git fer goin steady with a different girl ever other week."

I been thinkin a lot about reincarnation a lot lately, en ah figure ah used to be a alligator er a crocodile er sumthin er other like that. Sumtimes ah lay right by the water bowl with my hind legs straight out behind me along side uv my tail, en when the cats come up to git a drink ah pretend they iz deer er antelope, en ah snap at them. Our cat name uv Tubby, well he says he was a black angus steer in a previous life, en he kind uv trots around stiff-legged like them black angus calves do en he thinks he iz sayin "moooo" but he iz sayin "mew" in a high-pitched voice.

Old Tubby en Tweetums has been tryin to catch this here squirrel that comes on to our deck, but they ain't even come close. Them excited cats actually chase the squirrel right up the tree en they climb right after him except when they iz about twenty feet up the tree, the squirrel iz done up that tree en has jumped acrost nine er ten limbs en iz five trees over by then.

Tubby thinks he iz a computer cat, cause ever time Bob does any work usin the personal computer in that room where you stayed when you were here, old Tubby comes up there en lays down beside Bob en takes a nap. Yep, like Bob's frend Phil K. used to say, "Work don't bother me. Ah can lay right down beside it en go to sleep." Bob says Tubby en Phil was prolly related in a previous life. Actually, Bob says Phil was just kiddin around. Bob says Phil was always a hard worker, en he ain't seen no evidence uv that in Tubby; sew they prolly ain't related after all.

Oh yeah. Martha got one uv them Dutch lop-eared rabbits fer her birthday. It's a real cute bunny rabbit, en ah would like to flee it like ah do Tubby en Tweetums, but Martha yells at me en says, "No, no Sherlock! Don't you hurt that there bunny!" En one time she hit me right up the side uv the head. En ah just wanted to be frends. Ennyhow, Bob says don't worry about it, cause the rabbit ain't got no fleas ennyhow. Ah wonder if alligators got fleas?

Yore frend fer evvur,

Sherlock

IVORY HUNTERS WONT MAH EARS

Deer Unkel Gary en Aint Judy[15],

Guess What? Ah just had surgery on my, let's see now, was it my right er my left — yeah, my left ear. Well ah got this here hematoma in my ear. Hematoma iz a fancy veterinarian word fer blood leakin out inside your skin. Essept if they only called it that, they wouldn't be able to charge sew much fer the surgery. Actually ah got two hematomas from scratchin sum fleas too hard — ah just ruptured one uv them big blood vessels on my ear don't you see.

Well, ennyhow, the vetenaryen cut out two pieces uv skin from my ear. One piece iz about the size uv your thumb, en the other piece iz about the size uv J.B.'s left foot. Jan says that ain't true cause my ear ain't that big (as J.B.'s foot, not your thumb). She says one was a little teeny weeny piece about the size uv half a salad fork tine en the other one was about the size uv a Q-tip end.

Well, ennyhow the vet (he lets me call him vet instead uv venenaryen on a count uv ah am a good patient. He makes this here German Shepurd acrost the street, his name iz Shane, call him Doctor Wilson, Sir, en ah ain't allowed to say what the vet calls Shane, cause Shane iz real mean. Ah called Shane up on the phone one day en ah said, "You don't know who this is, but they ain't no sheep in Germany; sew you ain't no Shepurd . Not only that, you ain't never been to Germany; sew you ain't German. You are just a big nothin."

Where was I? Oh yeah, well sew the vet give me this hear

gas, witch wuzzunt too bad. Ah mean it smelled better than the kitty litter box en that smells pretty good. Actually, ah don't even remember any smell — all ah remember was takin a few whiffs uv that gas en the next thang ah know, my head started spinnin en ah could see the devil ridin around on a pink motorcycle wearin a chartreuse cape (the devil, not the motorcycle) that said "WELCOME TO PALATKA!" on it (the cape, not the motorcycle), en then the room got dark.

When ah woke up, ah was flat on my back en my ear felt itchy. By the way, you know how they say when you go into surgery they shave all your hair off? Ah was real worried about that, cause ah sunburn real easy. Well, they didn't shave you everwhere, they just shave part uv your ear on both sides. Ennyhow, while ah was asleep durin this here surgery, after they cut on me, they must have stuck my ear flat down in a sewin machine en put that sucker on automatic pilot cause ah got eleventeen stitches in my ear. The Vet said, "Ain't no blood goin to git in that pocket now, cause it's all sowed up."

Now you ain't goin to believe this, but ah got a thin sheet uv cartilage that goes all through the flap-down part uv my ear. Other words, if'n you were to skin my ear, inside there would be a sheet uv cartilage the shape uv my ear. Well, where the Vet cut my skin away, you can see my cartilage! En the skin ain't goin to grow over it neither — at least fer awhile.

Bob says ah better not flash my ear around too much er one uv them elephant hunters might think it's ivory en git me en throw me down en cut off my ears en sell them cause they ain't been able to git enough ivory elephant tusks. Come to think uv it ah ain't seen a elephant in a long time.

I been thinkin on how to cover up them cut out pieces. Ah went into Martha's room en was sniffin around her pierced ear rings box en had a pair all picked out, but she caught me en made me put em back. If'n ah can ever git Jan where she ain't lookin, I'm goin to try puttin sum uv her false eye lashes over where my skin iz missin.

I asked Bob if he would ever git a hematoma on his ear, en he said, "No, Sherlock, cause ah don't scratch my ears like sumbody ah know." So, ah figure the only place Bob iz goin to git a hematoma iz on his behind. This could be a problem on acuz ah don't think they make a sewin machine that big; sew ah told him he better quit scratchin himself back there.

Well, that's about it on this hear end. Tell Holly en Emily[16] Hi fer me.

Love, your frend forever,

Sherlock

TIPS ON TALKIN TO A COLLEGE MAN

Deer Leigh,

How R U? Ah M fyne.

Well, it's Saturday en it's rainin en Bob is watchin the football game on TV en Jan en Martha are out shoppin en Walker is out marchin around in uh band contest, sew ah thought ah would write to you on a count of ah ain't got nothin better to do.

How's school treatin you? Bob is always askin me, he says, "Hey Sherlock, what's the square root of three?" Sew if you figure it out, let me know, en next time Bob askes me that there math problem, ah can tell him.

Hear iz sum conversation tips when you are out on a date with one of them college men, especially if they iz uh upper classman, en you wont to impress them. First thang is to git them to talk about theirselves; sew here are some questions you can ask them:

How do you pass gas in the classroom without makin any noise?

How many times do you take a bath each month?

How much longer you figure you goin to be havin pimple prollems?

Can you blow a booger out of one nostril while holdin the other one shut with only your thumb?

What color would your hair be if you washed it?

A lot of college men like sports, sew here are some questions to git them started talkin:

How come the quarterback is called the quarterback?

How come the guy next to the guard on offense is called a tackle? He ain't allowed to tackle is he?

How come them football players is always pattin each other on the hiney when they go into the huddle?

How come they only number ever ten yards on the field? Why don't they number ever five yards?

How come the football field is sew wide?

How come they is only 11 men on the team? Why don't they make it a even dozen?

Some of them college fellows is into philosophy, sew here are some of them kind of questions:

Why do you reckon boys has more hairs in their nose than girls?

How come boys don't shave their arm pits?

Do jock straps have cup sizes like berziers?

Here are some cheers ah made up that you can try at the football game to impress your frends:

Cheer Number One:

Rah! Rah! Ree! Kick em in the knee!

Rah! Rah! Rass! Kick em in the other knee!

Cheer Number Two:

Chew tobacco! Chew tobacco! Spit! Spit! Spit!

Exlax! Exlax! Open that hole!

This last one is a cheer for your girls' dorm:

We don't smoke!

And we don't chew!

We don't go out with boys who do!

We can count!

And we can spell!

We don't go out with boys that smell!

We don't cuss!

And we don't drink!

We only go out with boys who think!
We got morals!
An that's for shore!
We don't git asked out much any more!

Well, that's enough advice for one letter. Take it easy en study hard.

Yore frend fer evvur,

Sherlock

ITCHY EN WARM BEATS SHIVERRY EN WET EVER TIME

Deer Brian en Janet,

We ain't been innerduced. My name is Sherlock. Bob en Jan en Walker en Martha belong to me. Here is a picture of me en Bob en this here nephew of Bob en Jan's name of Roger. Everbuddy says me en Bob is a lot alike sew ah will tell you that Bob is the one in the red striped shirt en his nephew has on the blue sweat shirt, except he ain't sweatin. So that leaves me — the good lookin one.

By the way, Bob says you all might be put off by the way ah spell thangs, en ah ought to spell in proper English. Well, ah ain't English. Ah am uh American, en ah will write in phonetic American the way it was meant to be done. Anyhow, you might have to pernounce words out loud to unnerstand them, you all bein from Wales en all like that.

As you can see, ah write pretty good, en ah know my grammar real good. Watch. Ah will now conjugate the verb "iz fine." Ah M fine. Jan iz fine. Bob iz fine. En Walker en Martha en Brother en Tubby en Tweetums en Buddy the rabbit iz fine. We iz all fine.

Oh yeah, Brother says he knows you all, but Tubby en Tweetums is two new cats that used to be kittens when we got them about a year ago. They is twin brothers en you ain't never goin to guess what color they are. Yep, you guessed it! They is black just like old Magic who died a few years back.

It is all rainy en cold today. They is a bunch of fleas in the house as always. So it iz miserable outside en miserable inside, except ah would rather itch en be warm than shiver en be cold en wet. Like Bob says, us results oriented individuals like to weigh the pros en the cons. En while ah would rather shiver than itch, warm beats out cold en wet ever time. So ah am inside en Bob en Martha are watchin the football game on the TV en Jan is in the kitchen except she ain't cookin sew they ain't no use to my goin in there for nothin to eat, en Walker is workin at his Ramada Inn busboy job en that's why ah am writin to you on a count of ah ain't got nothin better to do.

I guess it is pretty cold where you live, but it is real cold hear. It is 27 degrees. Bob says, "No, no Sherlock. Them people been away from Wales en Canada sew long they don't know about Fahrenheit no more. You got to convert it to Celsius. OK, let's see. Multiply by 32 en subtract nine. Then divide by five. No, let's see, uh, add five, then subtract 32, then multiply by nine. No, no, uh, let's see. Thirty days have September, April, June en November. No, no, that ain't it. Let's see…Well, near as ah can figure it, 27 degrees Fahrenheit is either 148 degrees Celsius or seven degrees Celsius, or Zero or somethin or other. Anyhow, my outside water bowl was froze up solid, sew you know it is cold here.

Well, anyhow, we got sum of your paintins hangin in our house, Janet. They is real interestin en nice. En ever time Bob tastes a good wine, he says, "Boy howdy, ah bet Brian would like this here wine."

Now let's see, where was I? Oh yeah. Well, here is the news about the family:

Martha thinks she made the "A" honor role at school this quarter, en Bob says, "So what! Ah made it ever time!" Onlyest problem is, Martha found Bob's old report cards the other day up in the attic, en they ain't nothin on there but C's en a few D's en B's, en a whole lot of teacher comments about how Bob ain't workin to his full potential, en how he could do better if he ever cracked a book en all like that. One teacher wrote that he needed to pay more attention in class.

Anyhow, Martha gets to go swimmin ever mornin at 5:00 en ever afternoon. Except some mornins she don't go swimmin. She goes to wait trainin. Ah told her ah could teach her how to wait on a count of ah am always waitin on Bob to come home from his bidness trips, but Martha said, "Why thank U Sherlock! That iz very nice, U wantin to teach me, but this iz uh differnt kind uv wait trainin. It iz where you work out with weights en build your mussels up real strong." This here weight trainin is supposed to make her swim better. Ah figure if she don't make it as a swimmer she could take that there weight trainin on over into bein a lady wrestler or somethin or other, but Martha says she wants to be a marine biologist en study fish en crabs en thangs like that.

Walker says he don't know what he wants to be, en it is makin his college selection a little hard. He is makin pretty good grades, en got inducted into the National Honor Society the other day, en he did real good on his college bored exams. Onlyest problem is he likes too many different subjects like chemistry en history en music en English en all like that, en he don't know if he ought to go for engineerin or liberal arts or what.

Jan is workin at the high skool where Martha en Walker go as a sekertary. Well anyhow, she does a lot of computer work on a IBM personal computer. En most days she comes home describin that there computer in terms that ah ain't allowed to repeat on a count of ah would git my mouth washed out with soap. Bob keeps tellin her that it ain't the computer, it is the program (witch just sew happens not to be a IBM program).

Bob is travelin a whole bunch. Last week he left on Tuesday en went to New York City to give a 45 minute presentation to some kind of conference. Dang long trip for 45 minutes of work. Then he left there en went to Philadelphia for a couple days. Anyhow he come draggin in here about 9:00 in the P.M. last night en ah give him my usual ecstatic greetin witch ah figure he needs after a long trip. En he always askes me the same question: "Hey Sherlock! Have you been a good boy while ah was gone?" En before ah can answer him, Jan tells Bob all the bad thangs ah done. She don't ever tell him about none of the good thangs like ah ate all of my food en ah slept good.

Well that's about it on this here end. You all take it easy en have a real good Christmas en a Happy New Year.

Your frend forever,

Sherlock

PUSHUPS EN OTHER THANGS AH AIN'T
GONNA DO

Deer Walker,

How is ever thang at Chapel Heel? Ah M fyne.

You ain't goin to believe this, but Tubby en Tweetie got into your room the day you left for college, en they was in there until about 8:30 in the P.M. that day. Now, the part you ain't goin to believe is they didn't wee wee or doo doo in your room durin that whole time. Ah know on acuz ah checked it out.

Bob tells me your roommate is named Mason. Martha wants to know does he burp or fart like some people she knows. Tweetie asked me does Mason throw cats down on their sides en beat on them like bongo drums like you do, en then Tweetie closed his eyes en started purrin when he thought about how you do him like that.

Well, Bob give me this extra special shampoo bath on Saturday night. On Sunday me en him en Jan went over to Lexington, Virginia to git Martha. She was over there visitin her friend Ingrid who moved there. We had to go over the mountains en cross over the Blue Ridge Trail en we was goin down the mountain down this here windee, curvee road, en ah was hangin my head out the window lettin my ears flap in the breeze, en Bob was hollerin, "Yaaaaahooooooo!" on a count of it was fun flyin down that mountain road, en Jan started yellin, "Bob! Slow down around them curves! Quit swervin! Stop the car! Stop the car! Ah got to throw up!" En Bob stopped the car. En Jan got out. En sure enough, she throwed up! En Bob didn't put no news paper down for her like he does for me or nothin, en she just throwed up right there on the grass. Ah tried to git a good look at it sew ah could tell you what was in it, but Bob said, "Sherlock! Get away from there!"

Well anyhow, we got to Lexington, Virginia, en Bob took me over to VMI witch is alphabetic for Virginia Military Institute. En these here fellows called upper classmen was bein mean to these here new college students. The upper guys were hollerin at the new guys. Makin them do push ups, en makin them march around en say "No sir! Yes sir! No excuse sir!" En all like that. En the most popular thang was to make them new college students (they call them rats) stand at attention with their nose against a wall. Ah figure they all would a got along a whole lot better if the upper guys had been tryin to teach the new guys more useful commands like Sit en Stay en Roll over en Fetch en stuff like that.

I asked Bob did they do that No sir, Yes sir kind of stuff at Chapel Heel, en he said "No, they just have these here girls in light blue shirts come out en grab all of your suitcases en thangs en take them up to your room, en they flirt with you en all like that." Boy them VMI rats better not find out about that, or this here campus would shut down fer good.

I thank ah will go to Chapel Heel. Bob said he didn't think my S.A.T. scores would be quite high enough for Chapel Heel, but on the outside chance they just might make an exception fer me at VMI, why don't ah try bein a rat for a couple hours since ah was there at VMI visitin anyhow. Well, the first thang you know, one of them sew called upper classmen got on to me about somethin en he had me put my nose against the wall. Then he said, real mean like, he said, "Tuck that chin in mister! Eyes straight ahead! Chest out! Stomach in! Hips level! Heels together, feet formin a 45 degree angle!" Well about the time ah put all four of my heels together en tried to make that there 45 degree angle, ah fell over! So ah stayed over on my back, you know, like ah do, en give that there upper classman a little wag of my tail, en he said, "Wipe that smile off of your face mister! En quit waggin your tail!"

It was bout this time ah figured maybe ah was better suited fer Florida State University. Bob sed he figgers if'n they R still usin uh two-headed coin in their admissions office, ah might have a good chance of bein accepted, but then ah wood be uh differnt kind uv rat—ah wood haff to root aginst thuh Florida Gators. Boy howdy, now ah see why U had uh hard time pickin uh college!

Well, tell old Mason hello for me, en ah hope he has a chance to meet me sometime.

Luv,

Sherlock

LAMAR GRIFFIN DONE GOT A STETHASCOPE!

Deer Walker,

How R U? Ah M fyne.

Well, actually, I ain't sew hot. I mean my temperature is normal, but I have had a upset stomach. I throwed up about four or five times today. Jan took me to the vet, Doctor Wilson. First thang he asked was what did I have to eat yesterday. This was the day me en Bob en Jan went to git Martha at Lexington, Virginia. Well, next thang ah know, Jan is tellin on me. She said, "Well Doc, he had his usual dry dog food breakfast, then he had a Hardees sausage en biscuit, en then about 10:30 he had a Dairy Queen ice cream cone, en then for lunch he had some fried chicken skin, en he had hush puppies en ham for supper en a piece of chocolate cake en some milk en a can of Vienna sausage en some chocolate chip cookies en some cheese covered broccoli."

And Doc Wilson said, "Uh huh. Well, I think I know what it was. It was prolly the sausage he ate with the concentrated carbohydrates in the form of a biscuit." En Bob said, "See there! What did I tell you! Sherlock should of eat vegetables en fruit!" Anyhow Doc Wilson give me a shot en said I couldn't eat nothin until tomorrow mornin. So I ain't et nothin since breakfast except for the chicken bones Jan threw in the garbage last night. I hope you are eatin better than that.

Oh yeah, old Lamar Griffin called tonight. He decided to go to the University of Tennessee. He ain't been there a week yet, but I guess he is feelin kind of lonely already bein sew far from home en all. He wanted to know what Judy Lamp's address was. Bob didn't know it, but he called information en got her phone number, en Lamar called back en Bob give it to him. He also gave Lamar your address. Lamar said he is goin to study to be a veternaryen en he done got one a them stethoscope thangs.

I asked Lamar did he have a thermometer yet, en he said no. I guess they save the rear-end instruments for the last. Anyhow, he says all the girls like to listen to their heartbeat with his stethascope. Course he has to hold it in place for them down at the heart end.

Well, I guess the first football game is a comin up pretty soon. I was studyin up on all the college teams, en I notice the only dog team is the Bulldogs. En most schools is got mascots that ain't no use to nobody like The Gators, The Tigers, The Yellow Jackets, en The Deacons. Seems like they ought to have mascots like The Basset Hounds en the Kitty Cats en The Parakeets.

Maybe you could git your school to change over to The Basset Hounds, en I could git a skolarship or somethin. To git the school to go along with the Basset Hound mascot idea, here are some cheers you could do for them:

Cheer number one (Do this one real slow):

Two cents! Four cents! Six cents! A dime!
We gone win the game this time!
We can growl en bark en bite!
Come on Basset Hounds, fight, fight fight!

Cheer number two (Do this one real fast):

Track em down. Put em at bay.
We gone win the game today!
You don't mess with a Basset Hound.
We the best team for miles around!

Cheer number three (Do this one kind of in between):

Rah, rah ree!

Bite em on the knee!

Rah, rah, rut!

Bite em on the other knee!

(Ah done give away the Rah, rah rass version to Leigh's school.)

Well, that's enough for one letter. You prolly got enough readin to do already.

Luv,

Sherlock

MARTHA'S RABBIT IZ A RUSSIAN SPY

Deer Unkel Joe en Aint Bobbye Nann,

How R U? Ah M fyne, en Bob iz got jock itch. For once, he iz scratchin more than me. Bob iz also hobblin around here with sore leg mussels on a count of he went dove huntin Saturday on the first day of dove huntin season, en he spent all day squattin down en hidin in a corn field en gettin up to shoot en squattin back down en up en down en his thigh muscles iz sew sore that he can't hardly walk en when he sits down he cries out in pain en when he gets up from sittin he cries out in pain en says, "Ooooooohhhh! Ooooh! Ooh! Oh! O! O! Auuuuggggghhhhh!" It iz real interestin en me en the cats always stop what we are doin to watch him git up. Anyhow he didn't take me on my long walk today sew ah figured ah would write you this here letter on a count of they ain't nothin else better to do. Oh yeah, Bob didn't git the jock itch when he went dove huntin. Ah asked him witch one hurt the most — the itch or the leg ache. He said he would rather not choose either one.

Well, Walker iz a college man now. He started a couple weeks ago. He come home this last weekend, but went back Sunday afternoon on a count of he had sum studyin to do. He talks in this here funny code language — like R.A. en D.C. en P.E. witch Bob translated for me: Resident Assistant, Dorm Counsellor, Fizzikul Education. Seems like the last one ought to be F.E.

High school has also started again; sew Martha iz back in class en Jan iz back at the school as a sekertary. So, it gets kind of quiet arround here. Ah ain't much into the soap operas en game shows on the TV. Mostly ah just catch up on my sleep.

Just afore school started again, Bob en Jan en Walker en Martha went down to Wilmington, North Carolina for a few days. No, no, ah didn't git to go with them. They put me in this here dog en cat concentration camp. There was this one cry baby dog next to me kept barkin the whole time. En when his master come to git him the dog said, "See! All that barkin worked! My master done come back to git me!" Boy, you don't git no dumber than that. Only time ah barked was when this here killer beetle walked acrost the floor of my pen. Ah let him have it boy. Ah barked him right out of my pen. It took about five minutes, on a count of beetles iz real slow, but ah never let up. You can't give them beetles no slack.

Guess what? Martha has a French lop-eared rabbit name of Buddy. Martha says "Sherlock, Buddy ain't no Frainch lop-eared rabbit, he iz a Dutch lop-eared rabbit." Well ah ain't sew sure. Me en Bob snuck in there to Martha's room the other mornin after she went to school en Bob whipped sum of that Dutch talk on him, you know, like he iz always doin with me, just showin off that he can speak French en Dutch because he lived over there in Europe for four years en all like that.

Anyhow, Buddy didn't do nothin. He just sat there with a blank look on his face. Then Bob whipped sum of that French talk on him en he STILL didn't do nothin — just sat there with that blank look on his face. Bob says he must be a Russian lop-eared rabbit! Oh sure! You speak a little American to him en he gets all hoppity, jumpity en acts real interested — prolly cause he iz tryin to git a American citizenship, bein Russian en all. He's prolly a communist spy or sumthin or other like that.

Bob went out to Santa Clara, California en also to Alexander City, Alabama (near Montgomery) last week on a couple bidness trips. But he iz plannin to stay home this week. Ah asked Bob witch town he liked better, en he said, "They ain't no Bar-B-Que in Santa Clara, but on the other hand, the Santa Clara folks don't care that you ain't a Auburn football fan; sew ah guess ah like them about the same. Although they ain't no grits in Santa Clara."

Well, that's about it on this here end.

Your frend forever,

Sherlock

THE FOREIGN LEGION AIN'T GOT NO COCOLA MACHINES

Deer Walker,

How R U? Ah M fyne, en Bob iz got jock itch again. Yep, he iz got it pretty good. He iz scratchin more than me for a change.

Martha en Jan done been to a Weight Watchers meetin this mornin. They iz already talkin funny about food — like, "That there bagel iz our bread allowance en this here chocolate almond ice cream iz our milk allowance."

Everbuddy except me en Tubby en Tweetie en Brother was goin to the beach tomorrow, but the weather forecast ain't too good. So they prolly won't go. Besides, Bob went to the dermatologist about his jock itch en the doc found a bunch of places on his face en arms that was what you call pre cancerous. The doc froze them en they iz now red, swelled up spots. Bob says they won't stay that way. He says them spots will turn brown en drop off eventually, en then he won't git no skin cancer. This has made a big impression on Martha. Maybe she ain't sew anxious to go to the beach.

Well, that's about it on this here end. En remember, you will prolly be burnin the midnight oil studyin. But don't try to burn the candle on both ends or you will git all run down en start gettin bad colds en the flu en all like that en miss school en flunk out en have to join the Foreign Legion en fight communists in the desert en hot burnin sand will git in your underwear en rub you raw en you will not git to shave en fleas will git in your beard en they won't be no under arm deodorant en big tarantula spiders will git up your pants leg on one side en killer scorpions will crawl up inside your other pants leg en they will build a nest in a unmentionable hairy part of your body until you try to remove them en they will bite anythang that dangles en you will have to drink water from water holes that camels have been drinkin out of en spittin in en they won't be no CoCola machine or ice or air conditionin for 387 miles in any direction. So don't play around with no candles burnin on both ends.

Jan sez they ain't no communists in the desert thet she knows of. She sez, everbuddy dun give up on communists en iz concentratin on terrorists now. Well, sumbuddy gotta worry about thuh communists er else they iz gonna sneek rite by; sew ah will keep watchin out fer them.

I been tryin to talk B.D. en Shane, them two mean dogs in our neighborhood, into joinin up with the Foreign Legion, but they ain't interested. They said they ain't goin no place where they ain't no CoCola machines. Ah asked Bob could ah join the American Legion, en he said he was all for it, but then he said they prolly wouldn't let me in on acuz of the hats they wear wouldn't stay on my head.

Anyhow, this Foreign Legion thang got me to thinkin about camels en how much they can drink en how much they spit, en would there be any water left at the water holes in the desert for you. So ah got out the encyclopedia en here iz what ah found. They iz one-humper camels en they iz two-humper camels. The one-humper camel iz actually called a dromedary, en iz real fast. Probably on acuz it don't have to carry around that there extra hump. When you join the Foreign Legion they iz prolly goin to give you a one-humper to start out with.

Well, this here camel bidness got me to thinkin about how you could use this information to meet girls there at school. The hardest part of meetin girls iz bein able to say sumthin intelligent the first time you talk to them. So here iz what you do, see. The next time you are at a party, you just walk up to a girl en say, "Seen any dromedaries lately?" En then you can tell her all about the two kinds of camels!

Well, ah don't want to overload you with all of my suave en deboner methods for meetin girls, sew ah will close for now.

Luv,

Sherlock

I LOST A SHOWER SANDAL DOIN THE HULA

Deer Granny,

How R U? Ah M purty good.

Guess what? Ah done had another operation. Now, now, don't go gettin all upset en comin up here to take care of me. It wasn't no big operation like a tumor on my ovaries or nothin like that. Ah just had sum cysts en warts on the outside of my body taken off. En also Bob told them to clean my teeth while they was at it. They done a good job on my teeth — took out the tarter en peanut butter stuck between my teeth en all like that.

Well anyhow, since your operation en considerin all the cysts ah git on the outside of my body, ah asked Bob did he think ah might git one of them tennis ball cysts on my ovaries like you did, en he said if ah didn't quit wee wee-in in the house ever once in a while ah might. Ah asked Bob if that's how you got your ovary cyst en Bob said, "No, Granny got hers from bein compulsive about cleanin the house en straightenin up everthang in sight; sew ah don't think you have nothin to worry about there, Sherlock." Well, ah went to Jan for a second opinion, en she said, "Sherlocky wocky (you know how she likes to talk that way to me) you don't have nothin to worry about honey baby since you ain't got no ovaries." Ah asked her if Doctor Wilson took them out when ah wasn't lookin, en she said, "No, it's on acuz only girls have ovaries." You know, Bob told me the facts of life pretty early on. Ah think he left out a few parts. Bob says ah should have taken better notes.

So how was Hawaii? Did you go to one of them loo wows?

Did you go surf boardin? Did you learn to do the hula? Bob says all the Hawaiians greet their frends with a University of Texas hook-em-horns sign witch, in Hawaiian, means "hang loose." Bob en Jan en I went to a Hawaiian loo wow party one time. Except it wasn't in Hawaii, it was over at Gerry[17] en Isey's house. We was just makin believe it was in Hawaii. Gerry en Isey hav sum big dogs name uv Benji en Berkley en Josef en they iz uh lot uv fun to be with. Bob calls Berkley "Barkley" on a count uv Berkley barks at Bob ever time he goes over there.

I wore one of them flowerdy necklaces en a grass skirt. Ah won the limbo contest real easy. Then ah drank one of them coconut pineapple drinks with the little umbrella stickin out. It was real good; sew ah drank another one en another one. Next thang ah know, ah won the hula contest too, en ah didn't even know ah knew how to do the hula, but it just come sort of natural after them drinks. Bob en Jan got sleepy en went home, but ah wuz havin such uh good time, they let me stay on.

Bob said ah come draggin in about 5:00 the next mornin wearin nothin but a pair of dark sunglasses, three shower sandals en a big grin. En then ah slept for two days straight. When ah finally got up, ah went outside en peed on ever tree in the neighborhood plus most of the car tires. Ah asked Bob was ah doin the hula when ah come home en he said it looked more like a sashay to him.

Bob has done bought a new canoe en he en Jan have already taken it out a few times. Once on a small lake, en a couple of canoe trips down a couple of rivers. They took me on one of the river trips. They found this here one-man life raft that iz really a one-kid life raft en when it iz blown up it fits perfect in the canoe en it even has a inflated bottom en ah fit in it perfect — it iz real good for sleepin.

Well, they iz a bunch of daffodils tryin to bloom up here already, but ah ain't seen no dead possums out on the main road yet; sew ah don't think Spring iz goin to be here for awhile. Dead possums on the road iz a sure sign of Spring.

Course, sum real big bass iz gettin caught up at the lake; sew ah told Bob he better git his boat in runnin order mucho pronto. He still ain't fixed it from last summer when him en Jan went out in it en the motor quit. Course he made this here trailer-dolly-cart kind of thang on wheels witch he has put the canoe on en he can roll it around the yard en park it under the back deck out of sight, en it fits perfect.

So ennyhow, maybe he iz goin to concentrate on fishin out of the canoe for awhile. They iz this here one part of the lake where you can't take a motor boat en Bob says they iz a whole lot more fish in that part. Ah asked him could ah go with him, en he said, "No, Sherlock, yore snorin scares away the fish." Ah figure ah will wear him down in a couple months en he will take me with him.

Well, that's about it on this hear end.

Love forever,

Sherlock

GOD DIDN'T NAME THEM THANGS LEAVES
FER NOTHIN

Deer J.B. en Lois,

How R U? Ah M fyne.

Well, Spring iz definitely gonna come early this year. They iz now three possums run over on the main road this week. Also Tweetie en Tubby iz gettin real interested in the bluebird box on one uv the tree trunks in the back yard.

Also Bob en Jan have been doin sum Spring cleanin. Ah don't know why. Our house iz clean enough to be healthy en dirty enough to smell right. It iz straightened up enough you don't hurt yourself walkin through it, en cluttered up enough you don't have to go lookin in closets en cupboards to find thangs — they iz out in the open where you can see em.

As usual, Bob iz way behind. He ain't finished his Fall cleanin outside. Oh shore, he cleaned the leaves out uv the rain gutters, but he ain't hardly raked up any leaves. Bob said, "Well Sherlock, ah was rakin them leaves up one day, en about the time ah got my second blister, it occurred to me that God didn't name them thangs leaves fer nothin — He wants peepul to leave em alone." Ah am always impressed by how human beings come by their religious convictions.

So ah figured ah would dig him a little bit. So ah said real innocent like, "Well, J.B. en Lois rake their leaves all up." Bob was real quick on that one. He went on about how that stuff that falls out uv J.B. en Lois' cypress trees ain't called leaves. So they got to rake it up. But these here thangs in our yard iz definitely leaves, en sew Bob said he ain't foolin with them. Then Bob went on to git out uv sum more rakin work by explainin to me that pine trees ain't got leaves, they got needles, en everbuddy knows you can't rake up no pine needles. Besides where do you think pine islands come frum?

Back to the spring cleanin. Jan got real busy cleanin out one closet. She was mutterin to herself en makin a fuss about clutter this en we don't need that en who put this in here en all like that. It kind uv scared me — Jan was soundin just like Granny. Ah was worried she was goin to come out uv that closet with a broom en come after me. So me en Bob snuck downstairs, got ourselves a couple uv CoColas to drink en four er five Twinkies to eat, en turned on the TV.

It iz amazin how interestin a TV program can be when you got a bunch uv work you are supposed to be doin. Me en Bob started watchin this here national spellin bee contest on the TV. They was a bunch uv junior high skool kids in this here contest. Now ah ain't takin away nothin frum them kids on a count uv they all looked real nice en polite en everthang, but the grownup was givin them the sorriest words to spell ah ever did hear of. Ain't nobody in their right mind would have any use fer the words they was throwin out there fer them kids to spell. It got me sew riled up, ah done looked a bunch uv them words up in the dictionary. Here iz sum examples:

Parturition—the act uv givin birth. Now can't you just see the doctor comin out to the waitin room when Walker was bein born, en the doctor starts talkin to Bob about parturition? Old Bob would prolly have said, "Part my what? Ah ain't got no itions!"

Tautologous—sayin more than you need to. Like tomato catchup. Everbuddy knows catchup iz made out uv tomatoes. But ah wouldn't go into a tirade about how that there tomato word was tautologous! Ah mean the whole tirade would be tautologous! People ought to lighten up about that tautologous stuff. Ah mean, if ah got run over by a car en Bob took me in to the Vet en said, "Sherlock iz bleedin red blood!" Ah wouldn't want nobody at the vet to slow thangs down by talkin about red en blood bein tautologous. Just git me on the table en git me sowed up.

Rickettsial—type uv germ. You know, if ah ain't feelin good en ah go to see Doctor Wilson about it, if he was to start throwin them rickettsial kind uv words around, why I'd figure he iz just tryin to jack up the prices. What ah would expect him to say is, "Sherlock, you got a germ that iz makin you feel bad, but ah got sum medicine you can take will make you feel better." Ah called Dr. Wilson up en asked him did he know about them rickettsials, en he said, "No Sherlock, ah don't sell rickets. Ah fix them. When Jan gives you orange juice you better drink it."

Coccid—a bug. Now how would that sound if ah was to say, "Jan! Jan! They iz a coccid in my food bowl!" Why, she wouldn't know whether to call 911 er take whatever it was away frum me on acuz ah didunt deserve it.

Procrustean. Now ah done read the definition two er three times, en ah still don't understand it. But it goes like this. See, there was this here fellow name uv Procrustes who lived in Greece. He was a giant. Well, whenever travelers come by his place, en said, "Can ah stay here tonight?" Since he wasn't no farmer, instead uv him sayin, "Sure, but you will have to sleep with my daughter." He would say, "Sure, but ah only got two beds, en you got to let me help you fit into one uv them." Well, one bed was real long, en the other one was way too short. Now, he must not have been too smart er else he was a real mean giant on acuz, to make peepul fit in the short bed he would cut there legs off, en to make peepul fit in the long bed he would stretch there bodies. Now after all uv this, you think you are goin to use that there procrustean word? Oh yeah, ah better write to Aint Peggy en tell her to not let Charlton go on no backpackin trip around Greece. They might still be uh bunch uv leg-cutter peepul there.

Incumescent—This here word ain't even in Webster's New Collegiate Dictionary. Ah figure the man callin out the words fer these kids to spell just made it up. See, this word caller man has been doin it fer seven er eight years, en he ain't real good at it, since he ain't got no accent, you can't git the spellin flavor uv the words he calls out. Ennyhow, ah figure he gets tired en bored; sew he throws in a made-up word ever once in a while to elimi-nate a kid frum the competition. It iz a pretty good system. No matter how the kid spells it, he can say, "No. That iz wrong. It iz spelled...(and then he makes up a different way to spell it). The other thang that lets this word-caller guy git away with it iz he ain't got no personality. You know, it iz like he iz frum way up North where it's dark en cold en wet en they iz only two er three days uv Summer ever year; sew when kids ask fer the definition uv the made-up word, he can make one up en you can't tell if he iz lyin er tellin the truth, en since he iz wearin uh suit en tie, everbuddy assumes he iz tellin the truth.

Back on that personality thang, one kid got hung up on one uv them made-up words, en the kid said, "Can ah buy a vowel?" En the word-caller guy did not say nothin, did not smile, did not frown, did not give the kid a dirty look, nothin. Yep, he iz frum one uv them two days uv Summer states. Ah tell you one thang, ah wouldn't want to play poker with that word-caller guy.

Cretaceous—havin to do with chalk. Yep, ah am shore Miz Sanderson would say, "Martha. Please go to the cretaceous board en do math problem number three." And, ah am shore Martha would say, "Miz Sanderson, ah know it iz sumwhat tau-

tologous uv me to say this, but last night ah had a rickettsial coccid; sew the answers to these problems were not parturitioned
by me. Please don't force me into a procrustean solution at the
cretaceous board."

I rest my case. They ought to just stick with words to spell
like "dog" en "kat." To sit sum uv the kids down throw in a
"Llaso Apso" ever once in a while.

Well, Jan done found me en Bob on the couch en the
Twinky wrappers en CoCola bottles on the floor; sew it iz time
to git back to work.

Yore frend furevver,

Sherlock

IF YOU AIN'T NEVER SMELT A PULPWOOD MILL THEN YOU ARE GONNA HAVE TRUBBLE FINDIN MY HOUSE

Deer Unkel Joe en Aint Bobbye Nann,

How R U? Ah M fyne.

Bob said he was goin to send you sum directions on how to git to our house. Ah figured ah would save him the trubble; sew here they are.

Directions to my house frum Florida by Sherlock P. Blanchard

I only took this here way once, but ah got a good memory; sew you can count on these here directions to be accurate.

First you git on this here highway where these two roads come together just past a house on the right where they iz a mean lookin German Shepurd layin under a big oak tree near the road. If'n the German Shepurd ain't there, turn left ennyway en git on the big highway—it iz called, ah ain't shore, either 65 er 95. One uv them iz the speed limit en one uv them iz the highway number.

Any how, you git on that highway en then you go to sleep fer about two hours, en then you will be crossin a bunch uv rivers runnin through a big wide open marshy, muddy, grassy kind uv place. Now if'n you wake up en see a bunch uv orange en grapefruit en coconut trees, you done went the wrong direction; sew turn around en take another nap twice as long to git to them rivers ah was talkin about.

So, along about here, you take the next exit after you begin

to smell the pulpwood mill. Pull into the back uv the MacDonalds hambooger place en git out en walk around the edge uv the
parkin lot en wee wee on the trash can en the telephone pole
en the rose bush. Watch it on that there rose bush sew your U-
know-what don't git scratched by a thorn. Now you git back in
the car en git back on the 65 er 95 highway. To do this, just pull
out uv the MacDonalds en follow the Ford pickup truck en the
old black four door Shivverlay with the bumper sticker that says,
"Don't follow too close — ah am chewin tobacco."

OK, now you go en go en go fer a long time en then you
start seein a few military trucks en Jeeps en this iz where Bob always says, "Yep, that's where Unkel Joe en Aint Bobbye was sta-
tioned a long time ago when he was in the Army." They ain't no
sign that says you lived here like a lot uv towns you go through
en they have a sign that says, "Home uv Robert E. Lee," but they
iz a sign that says "Fayetteville."

No, no, you don't turn off here, you just keep right on a
goin. Fact is, you are now 90 miles frum my house.

Anyhow, you go on up fer about thirty minutes, en you git
off where they iz this town. You will know when to git off, cause
just before the exit, Willie Nelson will come on your car radio
singin "Blue Eyes Cryin in the Rain." Ennyhow, you git off here
en head left through the town en acrost the rail road tracks en
right on up the road.

And you go over about 37 hills (I didn't actually count
them, this iz just a estimate — it could be 36 hills, maybe 38 er
39), en you go by this house on the left with a cocker spaniel en
two kids playin on the side uv the house en you go over a bridge
except it ain't a river bridge, it iz a bridge passin over another
highway en turn left en go down on to this here other road
witch has all kinds uv used car lots en a K-Mart en all like that
en then you git over to the left a little bit en you hit a few traffic

lights. The first two will be red, but the rest uv em will be green er orange. Up here, red means stop, green means go er keep on a goin, en orange means go faster.

And then you will see all uv these green signs hangin over the road with all kinds uv arrows en highway names en the names uv all the towns in the area on them signs en it iz real confusin; sew don't look at them cause they iz a easier way. What you do, iz you ask Aint Bobbye Nann, "Is this where we turn?" En she will say, "No." Then you drive on a little way en all uv a sudden, Aint Bobbye Nann will say, "Turn here! Turn here! Get over! Don't cut that guy off behind you! Speed up! Not sew fast! Turn! Turn! Turn!" Ennyhow, you just hit the gas en turn. This iz how Bob en Jan do it; sew trust me, it works.

You are now on the bypass; sew you can take about a 15 minute nap. En then you wake up en git off uv this road when you see three big white clouds up in the sky out to the left that look like the Pinta, the Nina en a big Harley Davidson. They iz also a crumpled up yellow plastic garbage bag en two empty beer cans on the side uv the road where you turn off to the right.

Then you go right en they will be cars on the right uv you en on the left uv you en you will hit a few traffic lights en then you will see this here tall gray haired man in a green joggin suit walkin his Doberman Pincher en you turn left en this rode iz kind uv bumpy en windy en after a few miles on a straight away, your car will slow down to about ten miles a hour en before it has a chance to speed back up, turn left, en then just after this yeller haired dog chases you, you will come to my house witch iz the third mailbox post on the right.

Well, that's about it on this here end. Y'all take it easy en come see us real soon.

Yore frend forever,

Sherlock

P.S. Bob done read over my directions en said they iz real good; although there might be a little more detail here than you need; sew he will be sendin you an abbreviated version in a few days.

IT IZ BAD LUCK TO OPEN A UMBRELLA IN A CANOE

Deer Lillian en Jiggs,
   How R U? Ah M fyne.
   I guess ah should warn you that ah spell phonetically; sew you will have to read this here letter out loud to git my meanin. Ah also ain't afraid uv no slang words like a lot uv English teachers ah know. They say it iz ignorance. Ah say it iz regional dialect witch ought to be preserved, otherwise we iz all goin to end up soundin like one uv them TV news peepul. Course, if we sounded like Walter Cronkite, that would be reel good, but he ain't been on the TV fer years en years.
   Even though we ain't been innerduced, Bob says ah would like you on a count uv you are both real interestin en nice, en besides, any frends uv J.B. en Lois iz a frend uv mine.
   Thank you fer the Super Duper home made dog biscuits. They iz real good. Bob wanted me to ask you can he eat them too. But ah done told Bob that them there biscuits iz prolly got animal by products in them like chicken lips en pig eye lids, en then ah said, while ah was eatin one uv them biscuits, ah said, "Yep! Ah think ah can taste sum castrated bull scrotum now. Umm boy! They iz real good! Don't you want sum?" En Bob said, "No, no, since you like them sew much, en seein as how ah don't always give you but one er two cookies when ah am eatin the whole box, ah figure you should have all uv them dog biscuits to your own self."
   Well, me en Bob has been doin a lot uv fishin lately. We

have been catchin a whole lot uv crappies, otherwise known as speckled perch in Florida, er Croppie in Minnesota, er Calico Bass in Pennsylvania er Sac-o-lay in Louisiana Cajun country (Bob says sac-o-lay means sack uv milk in French, witch iz a funny name fer a fish). Course that ain't no funnier than crappie.

Anyhow, in Florida, them speckled perch iz pretty big — you know, one er two pounds, but up here they iz usually smaller than your ear er my paw — no, no, that ain't right — ah mean smaller than your hand er my ear. But Bob has found this here sekert spot on the lake en we have been catchin the Florida-sized ones. Only problem is, it iz a part uv the lake where you can't use no motors; sew we have to take the canoe. That ain't sew bad, except the sekert fishin spot iz about two miles frum the cove where you put the canoe in. Well it actually ain't no problem fer me, on a count uv my arms ain't long enough to help with the paddlin.

The onliest problem fer me iz the sun. When it gets too hot ah ain't got no shady place in the canoe; sew Bob got this here special umbrella witch has a screw-down clamp in place uv a handle en he attached it up front on the canoe, en sew ah had sum nice shade. This worked real good while we were in the cove where we put the canoe it, but when Bob come around the point uv that there cove en into the big part uv the lake, they was a strong wind blowin.

The wind was a comin right at us frum the direction uv our sekert fishin spot. Well, the wind caught in that there umbrella, en as fast as you could blink your eye, that there canoe did a 90 degree right turn en started racin off down the lake in the wrong direction with me en Bob in it. Bob was in the back yellin, "Sherlock! Sherlock! Take that umbrella down!" Well, he knows en ah know that ah ain't the mechanical type; sew ah just hunkered down in the bottom uv that there canoe bottom en squeezed my eyes shut. En about 10 minutes later, while Bob was havin a discussion with God and Jesus, the umbrella shaft popped out uv the screw-down clamp en went sailin overboard (the umbrella, not the clamp). Bob retrieved the umbrella before it sunk, en he folded it up en put it away.

We was now two en a half miles frum the sekert fishin spot — Bob paddlin into a stiff wind. When we got to the sekert spot, sumbody had done come along en caught all the dang fish, plus ah got a little sun burnt. But it was a pretty good day en they iz just sumthin about bein out there on the water even if'n you don't catch nothin witch makes it all worthwhile. Plus we didn't have no trubble sleepin that night. Jan said it sounded like stereophonic buzz saws.

Well, that's about it on this hear end. Thank you again fer the biscuits.

Your frend forever,

Sherlock Blanchard

DON'T GIT UNDER A CAR YOU AIN'T BEEN INNERDUCED TO

Deer Aint Charleen,

How R U? Ah done been run over!

No, no — don't worry. Ah ain't dead er nothin like that.

See, it was like this here. Ah was run over by a car — one uv them Jackanese Toyotas. No, no, it wasn't Jan's Toyota en it wasn't Martha's Toyota. Ah was run over by a perfect stranger Toyota. Ennyhow, it was the mailman's car! Except she ain't no man, she iz a woman, except Jan said you don't call her no mail-woman, you call her a letter carrier.

Ah ain't quite figgered out yet witch all parts uv me got runned over — it all happened pretty quick. All ah know iz one minute ah was mindin my own bidness in the road in front uv my mailbox where her car was stopped. Ah was lookin at the inside uv the tire to see if'n there was a notice about not wee-weein on U.S. Government property, en the next thang ah know ah am bein attacked by the underside uv her car en drug along the pavement on my nose en then a spring shackle clonks me right on top uv my head en this here irregular car bottom iz grabbin me en tumblin me over en draggin me all at once. En the next thang ah know ah see the rear bumper passin by while ah am bein dragged upside down on the top uv my back en head en ear. En sumwhere in between kind uv like in a dream ah heared Bob yellin to the letter carrier lady "Whoa! Stop!" witch she finally did after she had done run over me.

Bob said he was real proud uv me on a count uv ah only

yelped out once at the beginnin en ah runned back to the house like a good boy. Ah told him ah was OK, but Bob called Doctor Wilson's answerin service on a count uv it was a Saturday afternoon en Doc Wilson made a special trip to his office just to see me. Bob said if'n he was run over, the doctor would prolly say "Well, take two assburns en call me on Monday." But no, Doctor Wilson, like ah say, he dropped everthang en met me en Bob at his clinic. Course, he prolly wasn't sweatin over his income taxes cause he procrastinated til the last minute like a certain member uv this hear household who keeps sayin "Sherlock! Get off uv that dang IBM PC sew ah can do my taxes!"

Well, they ain't nothin broke, just a couple er three skint places. The letter carrier said she felt the car rise up like a tire had runned over me, but Doc Wilson said my guts wasn't squashed er nothin. Well, like ah say, it happened too fast fer me to remember. Here it iz a day later en ah ain't got no sore mussels. My skint places iz hurtin witch iz gettin me a lot uv sympathy.

So what you don't know can hurt you; sew ah have got to be more alert watchin out fer thangs. Bob says ah am one lucky dawg en ah am livin on borrowed time; sew ah better be more careful.

One week later.

Well, Bob iz takin a break frum his tax work; sew ah thought ah would update you on my condition.

Ah M fyne. Ah never did git no sore mussels.

Now sum news about everbuddy else:

Martha iz over at The University uv North Carolina at Wilmington this weekend meetin with the swimmin coach en the swim team members. She iz goin to try out fer the team there in the Fall; although she won't be on no skolarship. Ah imagine she will make the team since she iz faster than about half the girls already on the team — she just ain't faster than any uv the girls on skolarship.

Martha has a job as a swimmin instructor en lifeguard here at a swimmin pool fer the whole summer. She recently earned her water safety instructor's certificate.

Jan iz doin pretty good. Ah thought she was only half way through her chemotherapy, but she only has four en a half months to go.

Bob has only gone fishin once this year (a couple weeks ago), en he come home with a whole bunch uv speckled perch (except they call them crappie up hear). Speckled perch sounds a whole lot more appetizin. He said he only had three dozen minnows, but he could have used up ten dozen if'n he'd a had them.

Bob was in Scottsdale, Arizona the other day on a bidness trip, en it was a hundred degrees! Ah told him he should have dug a long shallow hole in the shade, took off his clothes en laid right down in the cool dirt, belly down. He said he thought about it, but just went back to his hotel en turned the air conditioner down to sixty-five. He says you don't git no dirt under your fingernails that way.

Looks like Walker has a job as a automobile mechanic fer the summer — you know, doin brake jobs en tune-ups en replacin water pumps en clutches en alternators, en all like that. He will be workin fer Donald Stephens down at Stephens Auto Service, except everbuddy calls him Duck Stephens on a count uv Donald Duck. Ah only got one piece uv advice fer Walker: Don't crawl under no cars you ain't been innerduced to!

Well, that's about it on this here end.

Your frend forever,

Sherlock

BELGIUM IZ JUST LIKE NORTH CAROLINA, EXCEPT THEY AIN'T AS MANY BABTIST CHURCHES

Deer Martha,

I low R U? Ah M fyne.

Well, now that you have gone to college, we got what Bob calls the empty nest syndrome. Yep, ain't nobody here essept me en Bob en Jan en Brother en Tubby en Buddy. It iz reel quiet around here. Ah ain't heard nothin but classical music en a little Willie Nelson since you left.

Bob says yore roommate iz real interestin en nice en she iz frum Annapolis, Maryland.

Well, ah know you are goin to really enjoy college, en ah hope you git to make a whole bunch uv new frends. To kind uv help you with this, ah have made up sum answers to questions you might be asked; sew you will make a good impression:

Question: Where was you born? Answer: "South Florida." (Don't git too specific — it will make you more intruigin.)

Question: Iz South Florida near South Carolina? Answer: That's a very good question. No, it ain't too close. To git to South Florida frum South Carolina you got to drive about two hours through Georgia, then drive one hour through Jacksonville, en then drive way on down the interstate fer about another five er six hours."

Question: Do you still live in South Florida? Answer: "No. Ah live in Belk Hall now, en in between ah lived in Atlanta, en Brussels, en North Carolina."

Question: Brussels! Iz that in Virginia er Maryland? Answer: "It ain't in the United States. It ain't even in Texas. It iz in Belgium."

Question: Belgium? Where iz Belgium? Answer: "Belgium iz a country in Europe. It iz squeezed in North uv France, South uv the Netherlands en West uv Germany, witch iz why it iz sew small."

Question: Did you learn to speak any Belgiumese? Answer: "Si."

Question: Say sumthin else in Belgiumese. Answer: "Vous et une tete merde, derrier hole."

Question: What's that mean? Answer: "You have fertile thoughts en are deep within yourself."

Sometimes you will have to distort the truth in order fer your fellow students to be able to understand your answers. For example:

Question: What kind uv music do the Belgium kids listen to? Answer: "Mostly Willie Nelson, but sumtimes Johnny Cash er Dolly Parton."

Question: What's the Belgium Congo? Answer: "It iz a dance the kids do in Belgium. It iz a lot like square dancin. That's why they like Willie en Johnny en Dolly sew much."

Question: Iz they a lot uv Brussels sprouts in Brussels? Answer: "Yes. They all over the place. Ah used to eat them fer breakfast ever day en twice on Sunday."

Question: Do they drive on the left side uv the road like in England? Answer: The trucks drive on the left, but the cars drive on the right side uv the road."

Question: What iz the weather like in Belgium? Answer: It iz just like the weather at the beach in North Carolina, except it rains ever day en it iz real cloudy all the time, but other than that it iz exactly like the beach in North Carolina, except it iz colder.

Question: What does Brussels look like? Answer: "It looks just like Atlanta, except the capital buildin iz older, en they ain't sew many Baptist churches, en the town square iz made out uv cobble stones, en the Governor's mansion iz a little bigger, en they ain't as many picture shows, en they iz a few more restaurants."

Well, that's about it on this here end. Brother says, "Hi." Jan says be shore en eat yore vedgetubels. Bob says don't be sew busy gettin a education that you don't learn nothin.

Luv,

Sherlock

JUNEY WICKER'S MATH BOOK IZ GIVIN HIM WRONG ANSWERS

Priest, Hillman & Greene Publishing Co.
745 South 856th Avenue, Suite 96
New York City, NY 30201
Reference: Book: Practical Math fer the Ninth Grade

Deer Priest, Deer Hillman en Deer Greene,
How R U? Ah M fyne.
Ah M ritin to you on behalf uv my neighbor name uv Juney Wicker. He iz in the ninth grade again this year, en iz havin a lot uv trubble with your prollems in Chapter 1. He come over to my house to see if ah could help him. He says he notices when ah walk ah know how to put down three en carry one; sew ah ought to be good at math. Now ah ain't no whiz at math, me bein a riter en philosopher en all, but ah can see why Juney iz havin sew much trubble. Most uv yore answers in the back uv the book iz wrong.
Ah refer you to the problems on page 12.
Problem # 1: *"If there are 43 birds in a tree and David Brown shoots five of them, how many are left?"* Well, first off, David Brown iz a pretty good shot er else he iz not got his shotgun plugged, on acuz you are only allowed three shots. Alsew, me en Bob en Jan know David Brown, en he is not uh bird hunter—he iz uh commercial fisherman friend who lives on the North Carolina coast. Ah ain't givin no more information on David than thet on a count uv U might hand this here letter over to thuh game wardens en they might arrest him fer not havin uh huntin license, en they wood

tear hiz place up lookin fer that illegal unplugged shotgun witch he ain't reely got, on acount of U made it up. Where wuz I? Oh yeah, so jest fer thuh sake uv yore made up story, ah'll go along with David huntin birds. So, ah figure it must have been at first light when the birds was still sleepin, en David snuck up real close en got off three quick ones. Ennyhow, your answer in the back uv the book iz 38. Ain't no way. The practical answer iz either zero, cause they will all fly away about the time David gits off that third shot, er five (the five that got shot—they ain't goin nowhere). Ah think ah would also accept an answer uv no more than 10 on a count uv sum birds git paralyzed with fear when you shoot at them fer a few seconds.

Now ah will skip Problem # 2 on a count uv the even numbered problems don't have answers in the back uv the book. Ah guess that iz a pretty good policy, on a count uv how a lot uv kids, when they git a word problem, just take the two numbers in the problem en add them. That's one possible answer. If that don't match the answer in the back uv the book, then they subtract the two numbers. If that don't match the answer in the back, they multiply the two numbers. If that don't match the back uv the book, they divide the two numbers. If this don't match, they go see their daddy er their mama fer help. If it iz a even numbered problem where they ain't no answer in the book, it brings the children closer to their parents quicker.

Problem # 3: *"Mr. Parsons the grave digger dug a hole six feet deep, four feet wide, en ten feet long. How many cubic feet uv dirt will this grave hold?"* Now ah reckon you expect this here math to be practical en fer the students to do their research, witch iz what ah did. Well, first off, Mr. Parsons ain't like Mr. Albert, our grave digger, cause he says he digs the graves six feet deep, but ah measured a couple uv them en they iz nearer five feet. Next, Mr. Parsons must be buryin a perfessional basketball player er sumthin, on acuz ten feet iz a mighty long grave. Now, ah checked with my Unkel Gary who iz in the funeral home bidness, en he says the longest casket they make iz seven en a half feet long; sew givin a little room fer it to fit easy into the hole, ah figure Mr. Parsons actually only dug a hole five feet deep, four feet wide, en eight feet long. For the rest uv the research, ah called Mr. Bruce Moody down at the Belleview Hardware Store en asked him if he had a cubic foot shovel, en he said they ain't no such a thang. Ah explained the problem to him. En he said, "It can't be done. Even if you did have a shovel in the shape uv a cubic foot, the dirt would all fall apart when you put it in the hole." So the best answer ah can come up with usin this approach iz zero. How in the world you got 240 iz beyond me. The next approach was to ask Mr. Albert, our grave digger, about the problem, en he said, "That there iz a trick question! If'n you was to fill the hole up with dirt, the casket would still be up here on the ground, en then you would have to dig the hole all over again!" So, usin this approach, the best answer iz still zero. Ah think you need to change your answer.

Problem # 5: *"Farmer Brown has 43 pounds uv apples. If he sells them fer $1.89 a pound, how much money will he make?"* Well, if he sells them fer $1.89 a pound he ain't goin to make nothin on a count uv they are sellin apples down at the Winn Dixie fer $1.39 a pound! Ain't nobody goin to buy frum Farmer Brown. Not only that, he will lose money on a count uv his expenses fer fertilizer en the cost uv the marker pen to make his Apples fer Sale sign (I assume he will use a piece uv cardboard frum the dumpster behind the furniture store fer his sign, witch iz free). Well, since you don't give no figures fer the fertilizer er the marker pen, the answer iz zero. If you was a Republican you would have given the information about the expenses en also what Farmer Brown's tax rate is, en we could a figured out the real answer. How you git $81.27 ah will never know.

Problem # 7: *"Mr. Zanarini and Mr. O'Malley are riding together from Newark, New Jersey to White Plains, New York, a distance of 43 miles, to attend a meeting. If they drive 65 miles an hour, will they make it in 45 minutes?"* Well, ah got a edge on you on this here question. See, Bob, who ah live with, he has been to Newark, New Jersey; sew ah put this problem over to him, en he said, "Ain't no way. They iz eleventeen toll booths between Newark en White Plains, plus they ain't no way you can drive 65 miles an hour over all uv them potholes they got up there. Not only that, they speed limit iz 55, en they will git arrested. So, considerin the time it takes to stop en pay the tolls, dodge the potholes, en pay off the policeman, it will prolly take about two en a half hours." Ah asked Bob if they could drive the other way frum White Plains to Newark any faster, en he said, "Well, yes. **If** U R drivin a rental car thet U don't care uhbout fram-bangin in the potholes **AND** you are tryin to catch a airplane at the Newark airport. Why, you can drive them 45 miles in about 30 minutes if, say Zanarini drives en O'Malley keeps a lookout fer policemen en throws quarters in the toll booths as they drive by." So! To make a long story short, your answer in the back uv the book iz Yes. The law-abidin practical answer iz No.

Well, ah hope this helps you all, en ah hope you publish a corrected version before Juney starts the ninth grade again next year. If we can just git Juney up to the tenth grade, he will do all right on a count uv Miss Cromartie, who iz the tenth grade algebra teacher, only gives even numbered problems (where they ain't no answers in the back uv the book), en me en Juney can prolly explain our answers to her satisfaction.

One final suggestion: Y'all shore do use that there 43 number uh lot. You got 43 birds, you got 43 pounds uv apples, you got 43 miles to travel. Ah tell U the truth, ah think these children doin these math prollems iz gonna hav nite mares uhbout thet their number 43. It'll prolly scar em fer life. Why, later on when they hit their 43rd birthday, they will prolly all hav uh panic attack. Thuh football coach tried to giv Juney jersey number 43 en he went white az uh sheet en switched frum fullback to tackle so he could git another number. It'z uh good thing yore book was written after Richard Petty started racin on a count uv his race car number wuz 43 en he wood hav been uh nervous wreck. Sew please throw in sum different numbers. Bob sed U kin use his combination lock numbers: 14, 28 and 22, plus ah M 14 years old; sew that makes it uh double good number to work with. Fifty-seven iz uh good number. Ah like 57. Ah don't know why, ah jest like it, but U can have it. Sixty-three. I could give you 63. Ah got uh bunch uv numbers. Feel free to rite me if'n you need enny more.

Thank you.

Yore frend forever,

Sherlock P. Blanchard

GIT ALONG LITTLE DOGGIE

Deer Lynn en Sam,

How R U out there in East Texas? Am M fine.

Lynn, ah know U call her Aint Elizabeth on acount uv she iz yore Aint, but Walker en Martha call her Granny on acount uv she iz their Granny; sew ah call her Granny too. Well, Granny sez y'all R settlin in purty good out there.

Bob helped me look up on the PC map where you have yore cattle ranch. I thought it wuz nice y'all movin to Texas sew U en Unkel Hugh en Aint Peggy en Charlton en Roger wood be neighbors, but whoooeee, Roger wuzzunt lyin when he sed Texas wuz reel big—286 miles from where U R to where they R, en yuh gotta go through Dallas en Austin to git there! Ennyhow, ah bet it iz reel nice where U R.

Wel, now thet Joy haz used up her fast pitch softball skollership en graduated en finished en iz now uh college softball coach, ah wunder how many games U watched her play frum hi skool right on through college? U no, Jan played wimmin's fast pitch softball when we lived in Gainesville. She wuz the catcher on the team en the home run champ. Bob took me to uh game when ah wuz just uh puppy, but ah remember it like it wuz yesterday, mainly cuz them pitchers pitched thuh ball sew fast. Ah asked Jan if she wonted to pass along enny coachin' tips to Joy, en she sed, "Yeh, tell her pitchers to keep em out of the dirt."

Tell Sammy ah got uh bidness proposition fer him where him en me could be bidness partners. See, Bob en me wuz watchin TV today, en they wuz this thang on there about how wimmin

kin buy these here taser guns to pertect theirselves from muggers. Just az they were doin the demonstration, which wuz reel
impressive, with thuh guy gittin shot en fallin down en twitchin
en awl like thet, Jan come walking through the livin room en
sed, "so if they iz more then one mugger, the woman is out uv
luck, cause U kin only use the taser gun once." Well, this got me
to thankin about uh cattle prod! U kin use them over en over
en over until thuh batteries run out, plus since it is like uh long
club, uh woman kin give muggers the old one-two: shock-club!
Don't matter how many muggers they iz. Bring em on: Shock-
club! Shock-club! Shock-club! En sew on. All me en Sammy
got to do iz change the name frum "cattle prod" to "mugger
slugger" er sumthin like that. Alsew, if'n Sammy kin design a
holster thet would fit around my waist where ah didunt have to
carry thuh mugger slugger around in my mouth awl thuh time,
I could use one my own self. You know, have it where I could
reach back with my mouth en grab thuh mugger slugger out uv
the holster, whip it around en jab B.D., thuh mean yaller-haired
dog down thuh street with it. I could show that off at dog shows
en flea markets en we got us uh hole new untapped market. Oh
yeh, ah need Sammy to figure out uh easy way fer me to remove
thuh batteries when the mugger slugger iz in thuh house, just
in case Jan might git after me fer doin sumthin she thinks—ah
dunno whut—iz bad.

Well, that's about it on this hear end. Bob iz worried U
might go over to thuh Longhorns er thuh Red Raiders er thuh
Mustangs er sum uther Texas team; sew don't fergit to root fer
thuh Gators, no matter whut.

Yore frend ferrever,

Sherlock

BELGIUM AIN'T IN THE U.S. IT AIN'T EVEN IN TEXAS

Deer Walker,

How R U? Ah M fyne.

Ah bet U were suprized to find this hear letter in the UPS package. Here iz sum shirts that Jan has bought you. She says if you don't like them, then don't tear the tags off en to bring them home next time you come home, en she will return them fer uh exchange er a refund.

Here iz Bob's report on his trip to Belgium. First, Mister Swaine en Miz Swaine say hi, en sew do Rebecca en James who was a little baby when you were there. Paul Swaine who was in Lisbon, Portugal when you was there, well he iz in a bidness skool in London. Andrew, who iz Martha's age, iz in his first term at Oxford, studyin architecture en playin rugby.

Bob tried to call your old high skool buddy Roger several times, but he didn't git no answer. He says he ain't shore he had the right number ennyhow. They wasn't no Roger in the phone book, but they was a Juan R.; sew that iz who he tried to call.

They iz a house built on the vacant lot that was next to "our" house on Boomgaardlaan. The town uv Hoeilaart has done cleaned up all around the town pond en it looks real pretty. Everthang else iz the same at the centrum in Hoeilaart except the Dietz store where y'all used to git roasted chicken en bring home en eat has changed its name, but they still sell the same thangs, even the chicken. Oh yeah, Erik the barber has moved to a upstairs salon on up the street frum Stazzano's Pizza except acrost the street.

The Grande Place in Brussels still looks just the same except the buildins at the end where you en Lexie went to a Greek restaurant, well the front uv the buildin iz all covered up with scaffoldin en nets en they iz cleanin the front all up.

Well, Bob got to speak his little bit uv Flemish to a whole lot uv peepul; sew he had a pretty good time.

Bob said on his plane trip back frum Brussels he had to fly to Boston to git a connectin flight home. Well, yore old skool buddy, Alex? Well, his sister Jenny was on the plane, en Alex was supposed to meet her at the airport. Well, Bob had about three hours before his connectin flight, sew he waited there in the airport with Jenny until Alex came, witch uv course he was late about a hour en a half. So finally, way down at the other end uv the terminal, hear comes this hear dark haired guy runnin, no, lopin, except he seemed to make more progress side-to-side than forward. You know, his head was bobbin frum one side to another side as he ran. Well, Jenny said, "Yep, that's Alex!" En it was. Ennyhow he iz goin to Amherst en majorin in American studies en music. Bob en Alex tried to call you, but you had done left fer Maryland to play in the marchin band en watch the Tarheels lose another football game. Ennyhow, Bob give Alex your phone number. Bob says Alex looks just like he used to except he iz now about six feet tall.

Well, that's about it on this here end. Bob en Jan iz gettin ready to go to the North Carolina Art Museum, have lunch there, en then go to a picture show; sew ah got to go wee wee — outside uv course — en then tell them bye.

Brother says hi. Tubby says when you goin to come do the bongo drum beat on him again? He likes it!

Luv,

Sherlock

DEER SANDY CLAWS: AH BEEN UH REEL GOOD BOY THIS YEAR

Deer Sandy Claws,

How R U? Ah M fyne.

I mean ah have been a real, real good boy this year, Just ask Bob! Now if you call on the phone en Jan answers first, ah hope you give more weight to Bob's opinion than Jan's. Also, in case you check me out with the neighbors, ah just want you to know that ah ain't the onlyest one who doo doos in front uv Mister Wicker's mail box.

Now this here ain't no letter to beg fer no presents. Ah am sendin you my sekert wish list later, on a count uv Bob iz makin me put everthang in priority order. Ah done got the first 57 thangs ranked, but I'm havin a little trubble sortin out the other 112. Bob says ah ain't been that good nohow. He told me to cut it down to five er six thangs; sew ah figured ah would compromise en send you my top 125.

By the way. Have you got any Great Dane dogs in your neighborhood? They iz this one a couple blocks over where Bob en me go fer a walk ever mornin. He iz always tryin to play with me. Only trubble is, he iz young en uncoordinated en iz all elbows en feet, en even though Bob says he iz just a puppy he iz about three feet tall en them feet en elbows iz always crashin down around me. Have you ever tried to doo doo with a Great Dane jumpin around you Sandy Claws? It iz enough to constipate a fellow. So please bring that there Great Dane a rope sew his owner can tie him up er sumthin.

I hope you ain't mad that ah ate the cookies en milk that Martha left you by the fireplace last year. See, ah figure ah done you a favor helpin you keep your weight down.

One more thang. Make shore you come in fer a landin frum the West and land by the chimney. This way you won't be comin in over our driveway, en Donner en Blitzen won't drop no ploppers on Jan's new car.

Well, that's about it Sandy Claws. Ah love you.

Yore frend ferevvur,

Sherlock

P.S.: My stockin will be the real big one on the right. Also please give B.D. the yeller-hared dog down the street sum brains fer Christmas. He was neutered a couple months ago en ah think they neutered the wrong end.

SHERLOCK P. BLANCHARD, USED CAR SALESMAN

Deer Aint Peggy,

How R U? Ah M fyne.

You ain't goin to believe what Bob has done. He has gone out en bought a brand new four year old Ford Ranger pickup truk! See, it iz new to Bob even though it iz four years old, sew he calls it his brand new truk. It iz what you call a super cab. Bob says the super part iz fer me en Bro to ride in. Ennyhow, it iz white with a red interior. Ah ain't wee-wee'd on the tires er anythang yet, but it looks like a pretty good truk. It iz got chrome wheels. Ah asked Bob did them kind uv wheels make it git better gas mileage er sumthin er other en he said, "You wont to ride in this here truk? Then don't ask me them kind uv questions. Just fer yore information Mister Smarty Britches, them wheels en tires wuz on the truk when ah bought it. What'd you wont me to dew, take em off en buy sum regler tires en wheels? What dew U thank ah M, uh Democrat er sumthin?"

Since Bob ain't got rid uv none uv the other kars, our driveway iz lookin like a kar lot. Bob sed decidin whut to git rid uv iz hard. On the one hand he ain't got nerve enuff to sell the 83 Buick to ennybody. En on the other hand he iz just too emoshunaly uhtached to the old 69 GMC pickup — they been through a lot uv miles together.

Meanwhile ah bin thankin up sum ads fer the GMC er the Buick witch ever he decides to sell:

- 69 GMC pickup. $92,500 er best offer.

- Speshul sale on 69 GMC pickups. Sorry, only one to a customer en no rain checks.

- 69 GMC pickup. No A/C. No power steerin. No radio. No power brakes. This here truk ain't fer sissies. If'n you are man enuff, call 919-6408.

- 69 GMC. This here truk changed the rules a long time afore Dodge Ram thawt about it. Fer ezzampul, it don't like to git out uv bed if it's cold in the mornin.

- Rear window gun rack fer sale. 69 GMC pickup truk included.

- 83 Buick Skylark. Don't believe what Consumer Reports says. They iz just a bunch uv Yankees. Take pride in yore Southern herritidge. It iz your God-given right to buy this hear car.

- 83 Buick Skylark. Great furst car fer uh teen-ager who thanks they know everthang. This car will teach em a lesson.

- 83 Buick Skylark. Like new condishun. Fer ezzampul: The turn signals iz hardly ever been used.

- 83 Buick Skylark. Four tires, front en rear bumpers, rear view mirror. Too many other feachures to name. Call fer details.

- 83 Buick Skylark. The engine iz called The Iron Horse. The transmishun iz called a whole bunch uv thangs. But you can call it yours if you just call me. 919-6408.

- 83 Buick Skylark fer sale to a Christian family. Brothers en sisters, this car iz truly blessed. The owner talked to God en Jesus purty regler ever time he drove it.

- Four tires fer sale. 83 Buick Skylark included.

Ah told Bob, it iz too bad we don't live down there in the Ocala, Florida area, on acount uv Jan iz related to half of the South part uv Marion County en we could sell thuh GMC or thuh Buick to uh relative. Bob sed, he didunt think we oughta be sellin the Buick to ennybody we know.

Pore old Bob, he don't have one single cousin, en Jan iz got all uv them relatives. Aint Charleen mapped out thuh family tree, en it iz got about 30 boxes on each page, en there iz about eleventeen pages, back en front! Well, they wuz all farm families, en they wuz big families. Granny's mother wuz one of 11 children. Peter Perry, way up the line, had 12 children. He wuz in thuh Mexican-American War, en when he come home, people called him Pedro instead of Peter. The town of Pedro, Florida iz named after him, essept everbuddy pernounces it Peedro instead uv Paydro. That's how people know U ain't from around there if'n U pernounce it Paydro.

Whenever we visit down there with Granny, Bob sez, "Now, explain who iz related to who," en Granny starts rattlin off family names like Perry, Driggers, Remington, Waters, Smith, Hatcher, Lanier, en about ten minutes into it, Bob's eyes start to glaze over. Then, at about 30 minutes she tells about how Jan's cousin Rosamond married Jimmy, en Bob wakes back up on account uv him en Jimmy went to Ocala High Skool together, en then Granny goes on through two more generations. En after all uv thet, ah ask Bob, "Well, what do you thank?" En Bob sez, "Ah don't thank ah better bad mouth ennybody in Marion County on acount uv Jan iz prolly related to em!"

Well, that's about it on this hear end.

Luv,

Sherlock

WHEN YOU RUPTURE A DISK THEY DON'T FEED YOU NO POLE BEANS

Deer Bill en Ellen[18],

How R U?

Well, ah ain't been doin sew hot. Ah had a ruptured disk — you know, in my back. Ellen, U bein uh nurse en all, ah figgered U would wont to know about it. It happened a little over a month ago. Ah had a lot uv pain in my hind legs, and was paralyzed fer a couple uv days. Well, you know Bob. Nothin but the best fer me. He took me to Raleigh to the newrologist at the Vetenary Skool at North Carolina State University. Well, that there newrologist poked en prodded me en pinched my toes real hard en said, "Does that hurt, Sherlock?" Ah showed him what hurts. If his ear had been about two inches closer he would a known real pain, but ah missed. Makes me glad ah wee-weed in the reception area real good.

Anyhow this here doctor recommended what you call a conservative approach, witch meant keepin me caged up sew ah couldn't move around en don't do no surgery fer the time being, en my system might absorb the ruptured disk stuff on its own. So Bob left me at the Vetenary Skool hosbittul to see if'n ah could heal my ownself. Well, ah got to feelin pretty blue, en then one day sum flowers arrived fer me — ah mean a whole bowkay uv flowers. They was frum Aint Charleen! Well, let me tell you. Them peepul at the Vet Skool started changin my water dish ever couple uv hours en comin by en sayin, "Hey Sherlock. How you doin?" en all like that. Ah heard them whisperin that they ain't never been a dog git a bowkay uv flowers afore; sew ah must be real special. Well, it made me feel real good essept ah was homesick.

Well, ennyhow, sooner er later, Martha come by en sprung me out uv there en took me to stay with Doctor Wilson en all uv my frends at the vetenary clinic. Ah stayed there fer three whole weeks. Ah kept wonderin when Bob was goin to come see me, but he didn't come until the end. Nobody come to see me. Well, that ain't true. Dude, you know, Martha's cat, well he come to see me, en you ain't goin to believe what they done to him! It makes my hiney-hole pucker just to think about it.

They neutered him! Just fer comin to see me! CHOP! Just like that. No wonder Bob didn't come around to see me. Ah tell you, anytime Doctor Wilson come around, ah set down real quick to protect my unmentionables.

Anyhow, ah am home now. Kind uv weak in the hind legs, but feelin pretty good. Bob en Jan make me stay in the kitchen all the time, en Bob has built a ramp fer me goin frum the kitchen hallway out into the garage. It iz a A-number-one ramp too — all painted up en with a rubber runner mat en everthang.

Bob has done cleaned up en straightened up the garage real neat en everthang. He has kept it that way fer over a month now. He said he iz goin to take a picture uv it en send it to you, cause you won't believe it.

Oh yeah, ah also dropped a whole bunch uv weight while ah was stayin with Doctor Wilson. They ain't no table scraps er candy er cookies there. Ah ain't had no cooked chicken skin er no cookies er nothin like that fer a month! They didn't even give me no cauliflower er pole beans er pancakes! You know, beggin fer food iz a art form that needs constant attention to realize its true potential. But at Doc Wilson's they ain't into art. It iz all pure science. Ain't nothin ah tried worked on them. All ah got was dry dog food.

Jan has been on a diet. She has lost eleven er twelve pounds. You know, there ought to be a number called eleventeen. That'll be eleventeen dollars, sir. Ellen won eleventeen tennis matches. Bill lost eleventeen pounds. Benny wears a size eleventeen shirt. Sally walked eleventeen miles. Andy pole-vaulted eleventeen feet. Sounds kind uv good don't it? Let's see, where was I? Oh yeah, Jan also hurt her back, but it iz gettin better now, finally. Ah told her she could have come stayed with me — fixed her back right up, en she could have lost a whole bunch more weight. But she said she would have missed the cauliflower en pole beans too much. Ah asked Bob how much weight he lost en he said if'n ah kept askin questions like that the chances uv my ridin in his new four-year old truck were gettin more en more remote.

Well, that's about it fer now. Y'all take it easy.

Your frend forever,

Sherlock

ROSES IZ RED, EN CYPRESS TREES IZ BROWN: A VALENTINE POEM

Deer Malaine[19],

How R U? Ah M fyne. Except ah am itchin a whole lot. Jan says it iz on a count uv fleas, en Bob says it iz on a count uv ah am allergic to pollen in the air. They must think ah was born yesterday. Ah watch TV; sew ah am educated about these here kind uv thangs. Yep. All ah need to git me straight iz sum Head en Shoulders shampoo en sum Vaseline Intensive Skin Care lotion en sum uv that there PH balanced Sekert Deoderant.

Well, enough about me. Here iz a Valentine poem just fer you.

A Valentine Poem, By Sherlock P. Blanchard
Roses iz red,
And cypress trees iz brown.
There ain't no better kisser,
Than a big Basset Hound.
If ah could just be with you,
I would hold you at bay,
And lick your sweet face,
On this here Valentine's day.
Oh, you may think I'm teasin,
Or exaggeratin er lyin,
But ah would battle a tiger,
To be your valentine.
Roses iz red,
Except sumtimes they iz pink.

I'll be your valentine,
Forever ah think.
I know you don't mean it,
When you call me knot head.
I know you just love me,
But you scold me instead.
See, you ain't no different,
Than most girls I've seen.
In their hearts they really like me,
But to be coy, they act mean.
They are just tryin to git me,
To notice them ah think.
Like Walker's new girlfrend,
Says "Get away Sherlock! You stink!"
Well ah know girls feel lucky,
When time with them ah spend.
But it's time to bring this here poem,
To a self-assured end.
Yes, roses iz red,
And sumtimes they iz yella.
But ah shore am lucky,
To be your special fella.
Your frend forever,
Sherlock

THEY OPERATED ON MY BACK, EN NOW IT LOOKS LIKE THE S CURVE AT MAIN EN MAGNOLIA

Deer Aint Charleen en Unkel Buddy,

How R U? Ah M fyne. Well, that ain't exactly accurate. Now don't git your bowels in no uproar er faint er nothin like that, but ah done had a operation on my back. No, ah wasn't on my back when they did the operation. My back iz what they operated on. Ah had a ruptured disk. Now, now, don't worry. They done did it about five weeks ago, en ah am doin pretty good.

When ah first come home, Bob said the top uv my back looked like the S curve down where Main en Magnolia streets come together there in Ocala, This was on acuz uv they cut all the mussels aloose on one side uv my back to git to that there disk. Ennyhow, Bob en Jan had me in this here kennel cage at home fer three weeks, en ever since ah been restricted to the kitchen. Bob says ah ain't never goin to be allowed to climb up en down stairs er jump up on the furniture ever again. Ah bet Granny will be real glad to hear the part about not jumpin up on the furniture. Doctor Wilson says the S curve look will straighten out when my mussels heal.

I am doin pretty good. Bob iz startin to take me on short walks ever day. Mr. Wicker, one uv our neighbors, the one who has Shane, the mean German Shepurd livin with him, well he says, "My gosh, Sherlock iz lookin pretty good, but he seems to be hesitatin in his steppin out with his hind feet." En Bob said, "Well Jack, if'n your unmentionables were that big en as close to the ground as Sherlock's, ah imagine you would hesitate a little bit about where you put your feet too."

Anyhow, since Bob en me iz doin a little walkin, ah am able to write to you. See, this iz when ah think up all the thangs ah want to put in a letter, en when ah ain't doin any walkin, ah don't have time to think about these here thangs cause ah am busy eatin en sleepin en beggin fer food.

Now the real bad news. Bob en Jan ain't goin to be bringin me down to Granny's house on this here trip. Bob says this iz cause ah won't behave en lie down in the back seat. See, ah git kind uv nervous travelin en ah stand up on my hind legs en hang over the front seat en ah am pretty hard-headed about it. Bob said this would be too hard on my delicate condition, en besides Granny don't like me bringin down my flea collection.

Oh yeah, everbuddy iz doin real good. Tubby iz fyne, Dude iz fyne, Bro iz fyne, Martha iz fyne en goin back to college in a couple weeks, en sew iz Walker (fyne en goin back to college), Jan iz fyne, en Bob iz fyne. We iz all fyne.

Martha was head life guard at the pool this year en also was the assistant swim team coach. Walker has been workin the night shift fer a courier service deliverin en pickin up packages all over the state this summer. Walker ain't goin to be in the college marchin band this year. He says he iz goin to study this time around. About time since he iz a senior en needs to think about graduatin.

Oh yeah, Buddy, Martha's lop—eared rabbit who used to live with us, en then Martha gave away last year when she went to college, en then the little girl that had him she give him back to Martha on a count uv he was too much trubble to keep care of, well he upped en died here a couple weeks ago. Everbuddy was real sad. We buried him out next to Tweetie's grave. It iz a real nice shady spot, en they iz a lot uv grass all around; sew Buddy would like that. Tweetie en Buddy ain't never been innerduced, but ah think they will like each other en git along just fine.

Well, this iz a short letter on a count uv ah have only been takin short walks. Otherwise ah would tell you about how Bob en Jan took the boat over to the coast, stayed at their trailer campground en how J.B. en Lois came up to the trailer frum Florida en how they went out ridin all up en down the intercoastal waterway en the inlet en how they didn't catch no fish en all like that, but ah don't have time.

So, that's all fer now. Y'all take it easy.

Love,

Sherlock

AH DONE TOOK A PERSONALITY DISORDER TEST

Deer Aint Peggy,

How R U? Ah M fyne. Well, ah thought ah was fine til ah started takin that there personality disorder test you sent to Bob. Bob said it ain't no personality disorder test — it iz a psychological behavior pattern profile. Bob can call it what he wants. Ah call it a personality disorder test.

Anyhow, ah got to answerin sum uv them questions on the form, en ah got to feelin unconscious en em-bare-ussed en all like that. En then Bob said, "No, no Sherlock. They ain't no such thang as a bad personality type — they all have sumthin good about them, except fer maybe the category that Hitler, Charles Manson, Saddam Hussein, en a lot uv home repair en car salesmen iz in, but don't worry, you ain't one uv them types. Besides, all dogs go to heaven ennyhow. Well this got me to feelin a whole lot better, en ah would feel just perfect except now ah got to worry about this here big, mean, yeller haired dog name uv B.D. who lives down the street goin to heaven with me. Ah think most cats prolly go to heaven too — ah know all uv my cats will, cause they iz real nice. They iz this here one orange colored cat next door, he might not make it. His name iz Chester. Jan says just because ah am a scared uv a cat, don't mean it won't go to heaven. Tubby calls that cat Chester the Molester on a count uv he iz always comin over here pickin fights with Tubby, who iz one uv our cats. Tubby tells him off real good, but old Chester just keeps comin back en fightin. Jan says Tubby ought to do more fightin en less talkin, en maybe Chester would quit comin around. Sumtimes Jan iz a hard woman.

OK, sew here we go on the personality disorder questionnaire. Am ah a Outgoin type er a Introvert? Well, ah like to make frends with everbuddy, en ah wag my tail en all like that, en Jan says ah have a real expressive face, otherwise she wouldn't understand what ah am talkin about half the time. So this iz lookin like ah am a Outgoin type. However, ah don't go blabbin my mouth off if ah have had uh what you call uh accident in the house. En when ah am sniffin around in the yard er on my walks with Bob, ah just take all uv them scents in en think about them without talkin about it. Ah mean ah don't go, "Oh yeah, a rabbit done went past here, en what's this — a spot where another dog peed, en goodie, goodie, here iz sum cow manure to roll in." No, ah just process all uv that information quiet like. So, ah guess ah come down on the side uv a Introvert.

Next question: Am ah a Facts en Figures Man er Intuition oriented. First off, ah think you can be pretty good at both uv them, witch prolly means ah am a very well-balanced individual, but if ah have to pick one here iz my thoughts on the subject. Accordin to this questionnaire, Facts en Figures Man means you want the facts. Intuition means you can usually guess the right answer based on a hunch. Well, ah ain't real big on facts. Take history fer example. In 1492 Columbus sailed the ocean blue. Well, ah am a whole lot more interested in the correct color uv the ocean than ah am about the exact date. Everbuddy knows the ocean iz the color uv dishwater. En seein as how it was more than 500 years ago, a year er two off the mark would be OK by me. So ah would a wrote it: In 1493 Columbus sailed the dishwater sea. On the intuition side, when Bob iz goin outside, ah can pretty well predict whether he iz goin to let me go with him er not. Put me down fer Intuition.

Now this hear next personality category, they ain't no question about it — between Thinkin en Feelin, ah mean. See, Granny calls me a knot-head, en Jan iz always sayin, "Sherlock, don't you know any better than that?" Ah ain't exactly concerned with truth er justice. When Jan askes me did ah eat yet, ah ain't got the least bit uv guilt about sayin, "No, no, ah ain't eat yet! Feed me, feed me, feed me!" even though ah done ate about ten minutes afore that because Bob done fed me.

I ain't got no grudges against nobody — not even cats er B.D., the mean yeller-hared dog down the street. Ah git along with everbuddy pretty good — except fleas — ah hate them itcy bitey thangs, but Jan says that won't be held against me. So! Ah am definitely a Feelin kind uv guy.

Next question: Am ah mostly Orderly er Flexible. Ah am mostly Sherlock. But OK, OK, I'll try to work this thang out. Ah thought ah was the Flexible type, but ah never meet deadlines by a last minute rush. Bob said, "Yeah Sherlock, but that's because you don't never set no deadlines — you don't handle thangs in advance do you?" Ah guess he iz right. But then ah feel real comfortable in small, closed-up places. Bob said, "No, no Sherlock, that ain't the right way to look at it — you don't like to be cornered like the time Chester the Molester cornered you by the big oak tree. You didn't like that did you? Heck no! Yeah, ah guess ah am a Orderly kind uv person. Ah mean ah want my breakfast just as soon as me en Bob git back frum our walk, en ah want my supper just as soon as Jan gets home frum work ever day. En my days iz pretty organized — walk, doo doo, wee wee, walk sum more, then more doo doo en wee wee, en sew on. Then eat. Then sleep. Then eat. Then do the walk, doo doo, wee wee routine again. Then sleep. But Bob says, "Sherlock, they ain't nobody on this hear earth who likes to explore without limits than you." Ah think ah am decisive, but Jan says ah am just stubborn. Well, ah guess it ends up this here way. Ah think ah am the Orderly-type personality disorder. Bob says ah am the Flexible-type personality. So ah told Bob maybe we ought to ask Jan en Aint Peggy en Aint Charleen what they think. "There!" says Bob. "That proves it! You don't want to come to no conclusion — you want to stay open to other suggestions! That spells Flexible, Flexible, Flexible!" Guilty! Ah am a pure eyed old Flexible-type.

Well, that's about it. Ah am a Introvert, Intuition, Feelin, Flexible-type. Ah don't know whether to take a nap er go give the cats a itch job. Bob says, "Don't worry Sherlock, you got a Introvert, Intuition, Thinkin, Flexible- type watchin out fer you, namely me, en ah think them two personality disorders iz about the best combination they is."

Hallelujah en Amen — ah feel good!

Yore frend furevvur,

Sherlock

YOU AIN'T GONNA BELIEVE WHAT DOCTOR WILSON CHOPPED OFF

Deer Aint Charleen en Unkel Buddy,

How R U? Ah M fine. Well, ah guess Ah M fine. Let me tell you what happened.

Well, see, Bob en Jan en Martha went down to Florida fer a vacation en me en Brother en Tubby en Dude who iz Martha's cat who you ain't met yet, well he gives Brother a fit, but he iz real cute en cuddly. Well ennyhow we all went to see everbuddy at Doctor Wilson's kennel while Bob en Jan en Martha were in Florida.

Now, you ain't goin to believe what they done to me there. See, ah had kind uv been off uv my feed fer a couple days before ah went in there on a count uv my prostrate was all swollen up en hurtin. Well, Doctor Wilson, he found that there swollen prostrate pretty quick. You know, you would think with all the advances in medical science, they would have come up with sumthin better to explore your hiney hole with than a human finger.

Then Doctor Wilson started talkin about three possibilities en enemas en infections en all like that en then it got real complicated medical talk sew ah sort uv tuned out en started to thinkin about thangs like world peace en does God call his grandmother "Granny," en does God's grandmother call him "Knothead" like my Granny calls me "Knothead," en since there wasn't no start point fer time, they prolly wouldn't be no end point en sew have we done gone past the middle point already, en how come they named the milky way after a candy bar?

Finally ah heard Doctor Wilson tell Bob, "Now don't you worry. We will take good care uv Sherlock." Ah figgered that meant he was goin to give me canned dog food er sumthin.

Well, after Bob was good en gone a couple days, Doctor Wilson come in en said, "Well Sherlock old buddy, we have talked with Bob on the phone en we iz all in agreement that you need a little operation." Little operation.

LITTLE OPERATION! They done chopped off my unmentionables! Both uv them! CHOP! Just like that!

Next thang ah know ah wake up en ah am feelin kind uv itchee back there. You know how Uncle Hugh used to always scratch his crotch? Well, that kind uv itchee, en ah looked back there en there was my scrotum all shriveled up like a prune! Let me tell you ah took another quick look to see if my tally—whacker was still there!

Hallelujiah! Doctor Wilson missed it! Well, ah didn't sleep much fer the next few days on a count uv ah was afraid Doctor Wilson would come back en whack sumthin else off, but he didn't.

I was sore fer a few days, but ah am feelin physically OK now. B.D., the mean yeller-hared dog down the street noticed my deflated balloon bag right away en said sumthin real intelligent like, "Whut happened to U?" Well, ah told him ah was chasin Bob's truck down the street en barkin real loud en my unmentionables disintegrated, en sew he better quit chasin Bob's truck if'n he knows what iz good fer him. En then B.D. said "Duz it hurt?" En ah said, "Yeah, ever time a truck goes by, ah git this here excrutiatin pain." En B.D. don't know whether to believe me er not, but he ain't chased Bob's truck no more.

Well, everbuddy in the neighborhood says, "Oh, you poor baby!" En all like that, en it iz real embarrassin. Aint Charleen, U wonce told me when you have to remove a dawg's eye, they iz a fake eyeball U kin put in there. So ah was thinkin maybe ah could git Doctor Wilson to implant a couple uv them fake eyeballs in my scrotum en then everbuddy would quit feelin sorry fer me. Bob says ah have to have enough operations as it iz without gittin into plastic surgery kind uv stuff; sew don't go pesterin Doctor Wilson about no eyeball implants where they don't belong.

So, whenever anybody starts feelin sorry fer me ah just tell them about it real matter-of-fact en objectively like it weren't nothin. But Bob says ah am losin my credibility with my tellin uv the details. Ah said, "What, fer instance?" En Bob said, "Well fer starters everbuddy iz only got two; sew it don't do no good to tell peepul you had three er four removed. Second, if'n they was the size uv baseballs like you say, you wouldn't have been able to walk. En third, they weren't radioactive, en ain't nobody goin to believe you assisted in the operation. En they didn't glow in the dark! Finally, Doctor Wilson did not feed them to no tomcat—I don't think."

Oh yeah, this bein operation month en all, Bob also had sum surgery a couple weeks ago. Now, now, don't git your bowels in a uproar! It was minor surgery. Well, come to think uv it, it was on his behind, sew that prolly makes it major surgery — Haw! Haw! Haw! Let's see. Where was I? Oh yeah, he had a cyst removed. No big deal.

Well, that's about it on this here end. Y'all take it easy. Ah asked Bob if'n ah would be more lethargic since my operation. He said, "Dang! Ah hope not! Otherwise you will be in a deep coma 24 hours a day!"

Well, time to take a nap.

Luv, your frend forever,

Sherlock

BOB'S ON THE WATCHOUT FER THIRTY-SIX-FOOT LONG ALLIGATORS

Deer Aint Nita en Unkle Bucky en Michael en David en Jeff en Mark,

Well, Bob en Jan en Martha finally done got back. About time too! Dang! They done been gone all summer! Bob sed that ain't sew. They was only gone ten days.

Bob showed me this here article frum the Florida paper about a twelve-foot alligator that ate a ninety—pound dog on Blue Run down from Rainbow Springs near Dunnellon. It happened the very day after Bob en Jan en Walker en Martha, en Aint Charleen en Spencer en Granny went tubin[20] down thet very same river. Sew thet iz why Bob sez he didn't take me to Florida with him. This has made uh very big impreshun on me.

I asked Bob how much ah weighed, en he said forty-five pounds. So since that rottweiler dog weighed twice as much, ah figger ah am too little fer a twelve-foot gator to mess with. Bob said, "No Sherlock, that just means that you can be et up by any gator half his size er bigger. Well follerin that argument, all Bob has got to watch out fer iz gators bigger'n thirty-six feet long. En Tubby en Tweetums can be et up simultaneously by a one—foot long gator. Brother said he didn't want me to do no calculatin on him, en neither did Jan.

Well, Bob en Jan en Martha are bein real cool about it, cause ah figger they don't want me to feel bad about missin out on all the fun at Lake Weir, but ah think they had a real good time in Florida.

Bob said he rebuilt both uv the benches on Granny's dock en mounted that there spotlight under the end uv the dock en replaced four er five dock boards before they left. About time he did sumthin to help out around there. See, if ah had been there ah could have handed him the hammer en the nails, en fetched the boards. Bob said, "Right. You'd have been sew busy cuttin your eyes around lookin fer gators that you would have prolly swallowed the nails er sumthin."

I asked Bob what the difference was between uh alligator en uh crocodile, en Bob said a crocodile iz faster than a alligator. Ah said, "How much faster?" En Bob said, "Well, a alligator can eat you up in a second. A crocodile can eat you up in a split second." En ah said ah figured they would have to catch me first en ah could outrun them. En Bob said, "Sherlock, ah seen a gator run down a deer once; sew you better be wearin your tennis shoes whenever you go near the water."

U remember Johnson's Beach there at Lake Weir? U know, right there in Oklawaha, the pavilion built out over the water? Well, it is now called Gator Joe's en it iz uh restaurant en bar. En they have gator tail on thuh menu; sew Bob en everbuddy went down there en struck uh blow fer dogs bein eaten up by alligators by eatin fried gator tail. Ah told Bob ah hoped he et sum fer me too, en he sed he et uh purty good bit; sew he figgered he had me covered.

Oh yeh, another thing about Gator Joe's at Lake Weir. Ever month on thuh thurd Wensday, Ocala High Skool Alumni frum thuh 1950's git together fer lunch. Bob en Jan ain't never been at Granny's on thuh thurd Wensday yet, but they iz lookin forward to goin won uv these dayz. Meanwhile, Bob's classmates Claude en Diane Cruce send Bob en Jan pictures frum thuh luncheons.

Well, that's about it. Oh yeah, the weather here feels like Fall already, although it iz in the low eighties durin the day en low seventies at night. But compared to that there high ninedies ever blessed day, it feels right nice.

All fer now.

Your frend forever,

Sherlock

BOB DONE SOLD THE BUICK

Deer Martha,

How R U? Ah M fine.

Guess what? Bob iz done sold the Buick! Not only that, the feller that bought it was a college graduate. You would uv thought he would uv knowed better.

Actually, Bob got the old Buick all fixed up — ah mean everthang worked — everthang. Ever switch, ever light, ever thang under the hood. Everthang. En the car body always did look real good on a count uv Bob always did a monthly paint touch—up uv ever teeny tiny nick er scratch. En he waxed the car ever six months. En the interior was just perfect — there never was a rip er a tear er a hole er a stain on any uv the upholstery. Well, no stains except where ah threw up that time after eatin a bowl uv mint chocolate chip ice cream.

Well me en Bob en Jan went fishin last weekend. Bob didn't catch many fish as usual. Then he went dove huntin en didn't git no dove neither. He did manage to git his brand new used Ford Ranger pickup truck real dirty en scratched the paint in a few places. He has done got it cleaned up, but ain't applied no touch—up paint yet. Says he iz waitin fer the surface to git real dry.

Walker en his roommate Dave come home frum college Sunday night about nine O'clock en brought about three weeks worth uv laundry. This iz purty good considerin they ain't been gone but a week.

The toilet paper what your "frends" put up in our trees, what you call rollin? Well a lot uv it iz still there through rain en wind en all kinds uv weather it iz still there. Bob says it must be John Wayne toilet paper — rough en tough en won't take no crap off uv nobody. Haw, haw, haw! That's a joke J.B. told us one time.

Bob put out fertilizer on the yard last Friday night. Then while he was off fishin John come around en mowed the lawn with his super vacuum sucker—upper lawn mower en sucked up most uv the fertilizer when he cut the grass.

Well, that's about it on this here end.

Luv forever,

Sherlock

THE BOOGER MAN EN CHESTER THE MOLESTER

Deer Granny en Papa Bruce[21],

How R U? Ah M fyne.

I am sendin you this here video tape that Bob has made. Ah also am sendin a copy to J.B. en Lois sew you don't have to worry about them gettin it.

Well, they ain't a whole lot uv news on a count uv Bob done got it all on the tape.

Oh yeah, Jan left me alone in the kitchen the other day while she went to the store er sumthin er other real quick. Well ah got in the garbage. Parts uv it were real good, except fer the coffee grounds en the wilted lettuce en the onion skins. En ah was pretty good about it. You know, usually, ah spread it all around in the livin room en the dinin room en the kitchen; sew ah don't have to deal with all uv it at once, but this time ah just spread it all over the kitchen. You know, ah like to help out whenever ah can.

Well, when Jan got back she got real mad at me en called me worse thangs than you call me, Granny. Well, as soon as ah could position myself under the bed en ah could reason with her ah told her she should forgive me on a count uv ah am only human. Well, she didn't buy that their argument; sew ah give her that line about catchin more flies with honey than with vinegar, en she said, "I wished you was a fly — matter uv fact ah am goin to git my tennis racket en use it fer a fly swatter!" Ah wish Joe en Ginny[22] had their flower shop up here instead uv in Belleview sew ah could git sum flowers frum them en give em to Jan to calm things down sum.

I don't know. You try to be considerate, but there just ain't no pleasin sum peepul. Jan ain't never give me no credit fer drinkin out uv the toilet bowl sew she don't have to put out a water bowl fer me. She just keeps puttin fresh water in the water bowl ever day ennyway.

Bob has put in these here outdoor walkway lights that come on automatically when it starts gettin dark en then turn off around midnight. They iz real neat, en Bob says ah don't have to worry about gettin electrocuted when ah wee wee on them on a count uv they iz low voltage, whatever that means. Ah like them because now the booger man can't hide in the bushes by our sidewalk.

Before Bob put them lights out there, ah was walkin down the sidewalk comin back to the house after doin my bidness one night. They wasn't no moon out. Ah mean it was pitch dark. Well, ah had the sniffles; sew ah got to wonderin if boogers have any vitamins er minerals in them, en that got me to thinkin about the booger man, witch has nothin to do with boogers, they just sound the same.

Everbuddy knows about the booger man. The kids in the neighborhood talk about him all the time when it gets dark out. Ah was thinkin how the booger man catches you en rips your arms out en tears your guts out en chews your neck off. Just then our cat Tubby jumped out uv the bushes at me, en was gone in a flash, but not before ah done my bidness all over again right there on the sidewalk. It's a good thang Bob was watchin — that way ah didn't git in trubble fer the mess.

Later on, Tubby come on in the house just strollin around en purrin like he didn't do nothin. Ever since then, Bob has been callin Tubby "Booger Man." I'd like to Booger Man him.

I been sort uv reluctant to go outside en do my nightly constitutional ever since the Tubby Booger Man thang; sew Bob has done gone state-of-the-art on outdoor lights. Our spotlights that shine down our driveway iz got this here electric heat sensor, motion detector, light sensor eye; sew at night when you walk out uv the garage er a car comes in the driveway er the neighbors cat walks acrost the driveway er when ah walk past the corner uv the house, the floodlights turn on until that there electronic eye don't see you no more, en then it turns off.

Only problem is, they iz sum times at night when ah ain't out there, they ain't no cats er other dogs out there, en they ain't no cars drivin down the driveway en the flood lights come on. Bob says he can't figure it out. Can't figure it out! Can't figure it out? Bob ain't puttin two en two together. It's the booger man! En ah doant mean Tubby.

This here neighbor's cat his name iz Chester (the molester), well he likes the electronic light turner-oner thang, en he comes over en makes it turn on two er three times a week. Ennyhow, Chester iz real dark orange colored with long hair, witch ah figure iz fer perfection when he gets in fights (the long part, not the orange part).

Well, ah was over in Chester The Molester's yard the other day fertilizin sum uv their border grass, en this here Chester comes right towards me doin a combat Rambo crawl en his eyes were real wild lookin en he was makin this here miniature air raid siren sound inside his throat with his mouth closed. Well ah looked back behind me in case ah needed to run alert Bob about this here situation. When ah turned my head back around ah figured ah would curl my top lip back en show Chester sum teeth — you know, not much, just enough to put him in his place — let him know who he was dealin with. Ah brung my head back around to confront Chester.

The killer wasn't no more than four inches frum my face! He opened up his mouth. His three-inch fangs were drippin with poison! He let that there air raid siren blast right in my face! Later on, Bob said it looked like ah was doin a swimmers flip turn, the side stroke, the back stroke en the butterfly stroke all at once. Not only that, Bob said once ah got back in my own yard en told Chester off, ah was barkin in soprano.

Well, that's about it on this here end. Ah hope you enjoy the video. One thang — ah ain't as fat as that there video makes me look. Bob says that's because ah am tri-colored; sew ah have been thinkin about dyin my hair — maybe purple, but Bob said if'n he'd a wanted a purple basset hound he'd have got one. Well, ah guess I'll just have to stay natural fer awhile.

Luv,

Sherlock

SHERLOCK'S BOOK UV FAMILY WORLD RECORDS

Deer Jimmy en Dee Ann[23],

How R U? Ah M fyne.

They iz a video tape a makin the rounds witch will git to you eventually. It has most uv the news; sew ah ain't got a whole lot uv news.

Tubby en Tweety, our cats you know? Well maybe you know Tweety by his proper name uv Tweetums. Well ennyhow, they iz both got a upper respiratory infection en iz havin to take pills ever day twice a day. Tubby iz a better pill taker than Tweety. Ah even take a pill better than Tweety.

This got me to thinkin about who does what best. Ah have come up with Sherlock's Book uv Family World Records. Well, it ain't actually a book yet. Ah just wrote it down. Here it is.

Introduction

I will list everbuddy by rank order. Example: I. means first place, 2. means second place, 3. means third place en sew on.

If they iz a tie, ah will list both names on the same line. For example, in the category uv most feet, they iz a four way tie fer first place, en sew ah would have:

I. Brother, Sherlock, Tubby en Tweety.

Sometimes not everbuddy will be listed in the rank order on a count uv they ain't got enough experience. For example, in the Best Kisser category ah don't list Brother, Tubby er Tweety.

And sumtimes not everbuddy will be listed in the rank order on a count uv they ain't no good at it. For example, in the Best Snorer category, Tubby en Tweety ain't included.

Personal Behavior

Best burper

1. Bob

Best alternate passage burper

1. Bob

2. Sherlock

Most nose hairs

This iz a trick category on a count uv boys iz got more nose hairs than girls.

1. Sherlock

2. Bob en Walker

3. Brother, Tubby en Tweety

Best Cooker uv sweet puhtaters, collard greens, pole beans, en squash

1. Jan

2. Jan

3. Jan

Most reguler member uv the clean-plate club

1. Sherlock

2. Bob

Messiest room

1. Martha

2. Bob en Jan

3. Walker

Spookiest

1. Tubby en Tweety

2. Brother

3. Martha

Best sleeper

1. Sherlock

2. Brother

3. Tubby en Tweety

Best snorer
1. Sherlock
2. Bob
3. Jan
4. Brother

Best greeter at the door
1. Sherlock

Best barker
1. Sherlock
2. Jan

Best smeller uv strange odors
1. Sherlock
2. Martha (especially alternate passage burps)

Best dansers
1. Bob en Jan
2. Sherlock
3. Martha, Walker

Faverit song
Bob: On the Road Again.
Jan: Anythang by Billy Joel.
Walker en Martha: Sum kind uv loud stuff.
Brother, Tubby en Tweety: Three Blind Mice.
Sherlock: Mozart's Symphony No. 41 in C-Major en the Happy Birthday song.

Dominunt obseshunn
Bob: Fishin lures.
Jan: Chocolate en shoppin malls.
Walker: Fixin thangs that ain't broke on the Mustang.
Martha: Competitive swimmin.
Sherlock: Worryin about starvin to death.
Brother: Sulkin.

Tubby: Gettin a daily itch job.

Tweety: Chewin up the rubber straps on Martha's swim goggles.

Things most scared of

Bob: Cockroaches.

Jan: Spiders.

Walker: Will Ford discontinue makin 64 Mustang parts?

Martha: Spiders.

Sherlock: Starvin to death.

Brother: Outside.

Tubby en Tweety: The doorbell.

Automotive

Best cusser while workin on the car

1. Bob
2. Martha
3. Walker

Most speedin tickets

1. Bob (3)
2. Martha (1)

Biggest gas bill

1. Martha
2. Jan
3. Walker (when he iz home frum college)
4. Bob

Sports

Best wrestler on the floor

1. Sherlock
2. Bob

Best dog paddle (swimmin)

1. Sherlock
2. Bob
3. Jan

Best butterfly swim stroke
1. Martha
2. Walker

Fastest freestyle swimmer
1. Martha en Walker
2. Bob
3. Jan

Fastest freestyle swimmer when Bob yells, "Alligator!"
1. Sherlock

Fastest getter-outer uv the water once in
1. Brother, Tubby, en Tweetums
2. Jan
3. Sherlock

Fastest getter-inner in the water
1. Bob
2. Martha

Biggest splash when divin
1. Bob
2. Bob
3. Bob

Well, that's all thuh records ah hav recorded fer now. Maybe more later.

Luv,

Sherlock

THE LAWN MOWER EN THE SPIDER

Deer Unkel Gary en Aint Judy,

How R U? Ah M fyne.

Well, thuh old lawnmower gave up the ghost after 10 years. So Bob said it was time to git a new one.

Jan asked Bob, "What kind are you goin to get?"

"I don't know." says Bob, "I thought ah would go down to the library en do sum research. It's a very good library, en ah am shore they even have Consumer Reports publications witch rate the various lawn mowers. They're open till 9 PM."

"I mean what features?" says Jan.

"Well, you got your motor, you got your blade that goes round en round, en you push it. They're pretty simple."

"What about self-propelled?" askes Jan.

"Self propelled! Who needs self propelled? They ain't that hard to push!"

Boy howdy. This was gettin interestin. Ah started listenin real good to Bob en Jan discussin this here new lawn mower they ain't got yet.

So Jan says, "Well it hurts my back to push a mower, especially on the hills."

"Hills! What hills?" Bob demanded to know. He was usin the tone uv voice he uses with me when ah am beggin fer food, en he says, "Food? What food? Sherlock, you just ate!"

So Jan says — she says, "Around the culvert on both sides uv the drive, en the big down-hill slope area to the left uv our front door where all the grass iz growin."

"Oh." says Bob. "Well, a self-propelled mower costs a lot more, en they iz just that much more to break, en ah never have liked them ennyhow. Ah don't think the non-self-propelled ones are that hard to push. Self-propelled ones are dangerous. They can git away frum you."

Jan says, "Well I'm shore they all have kill switches these days; sew they won't run away frum you. But it's not worth arguin about. It sounds like you are goin to git what you want ennyway." Her words are heavy-like. She has a look on her face like ah do when Bob says ah can't go with him in the truck — wherever he iz goin.

Bob gives me a wink when Jan ain't lookin. Ah can tell he has decided on a good strategy. He iz goin to drop the conversation, en not go fer the final victory right now. He will let it what you call incubate overnight. She'll come around.

I've got to hand it to Bob. When he debates a point uv view it iz a clear, obvious, spontaneous utterance uv logic en truth — It's a natural thang fer him. It iz inside. He just opens his mouth, en sumhow out come the iron-clad points, the right answers. Anybody can do it. With a little self-confidence en enthusiasm you will win!

Dawn breaks. Jan iz already up en gettin ready fer work. So Bob who iz still layin in bed, invites me up on the bed with him. He pulls me over to him en gives me a hug en a wink. He iz about to show me how to go fer the kill. "Well, Deer, do you feel better about my decision not to git a self-propelled mower?" (Bob says this technique iz called the trial close — Jan may agree, en Bob don't have to put forward no more shore-fire arguments in favor uv a non-self-propelled mower).

"Well, ah just have a few questions," says Jan:

"How long do you expect a new mower to last?" "Oh, seven er eight years."

"How much more does a self-propelled mower cost?" "Oh, $500 dollars." (Bob winks at me. Ah can tell he iz exaggeratin to close this loophole, heh, heh, heh).

"So, we'll use the mower 25—30 times a year fer 7 er 8 years, en a self-propelled mower iz only $500 more." (I start to do the arithmetic mentally on how much it iz per lawn cuttin, but Jan takes a more direct route…)

"So you paid all that money fer a big new outboard motor two years ago that you have used less than ten times a year. En you spent more than $500 on a new shotgun last year, en you already had three perfectly good shotguns. You don't go huntin more than 10 times a year. En you are not goin to spend $500 on a mower that ah will be able to use fer 7 er 8 years without hurtin my back when you are off on a bidness trip er huntin er fishin!" (She said it with a ! but she meant ???????? !!!!!!!!!!).

Oh, Bob started in with those knee-jerk counter-arguments about comparin apples en oranges; since outboards en shotguns are toys, en…Bob stopped talkin in mid-sentence. Jan, who hates spiders (but understands their ways), once again has waited, has let Bob spin his own web, en he iz trapped in it. They ain't no escape.

Later on ah asked Jan how come Bob ain't never won a argument with her. En she sed, "Sherlocky Wocky, honey, that's because ah only choose to argue with Bob on certain types uv conclusions he has made." Ah asked her which kinds uv conclusions those were, en she sed, "Why, it iz those conclusions Bob has reached before he has actually got to them."

We iz now the proud owner uv a new self-propelled lawnmower. En no, it wasn't anywhere near as much as $500 more.

P.S. It has a kill-switch.

Well, that's all the news on this hear end. Tell Holly en

Emily en Gary en Randy en Emma en Bethany en Griffin en Brock hello fer me.

Luv,

Sherlock

HOW TO PICK A COLLEGE

Deer Roger,
How R you? Ah M fyne.
Aint Peggy said you were havin a lot uv trubble pickin out a college. Ah know Walker had a lot uv trubble too; sew ah helped him with his selection process. The main thang you got to do iz read between the lines uv them slick glossy brochures them college's send you. Here iz sum uv the thangs me en Walker learned frum our experience.
What The Brochures Say
What They Mean
Bicycle racks are conveniently located throughout the campus.
You ain't goin to be allowed to have a car on campus.
The college, because uv its location, enjoys a pleasant climate.
It ain't never snowed here in July.
The townspeople appreciate the special relationship they have with the college.
Store owners jack up the prices when skool iz in session.
Classical architecture.
The buildins iz built out uv old bricks.
Convenient to public transportation.
There iz a bunch uv railroad tracks runnin right by the dorms.
Quiet campus.
There iz a grave yard acrost the street.
In a rural settin.

It iz down wind frum a pig farm.

The campus cafeteria offers an assortment uv well-balanced meals.

You can have koolaid or tea with your grits.

Friendly, approachable faculty.

Most uv the professors iz homosexuals.

A variety uv extra-curricular activities are available.

They iz a bunch uv pool halls borderin the campus.

Spacious dorm rooms.

Ceilins are twelve feet high instead uv eight feet high.

Classrooms are air-conditioned.

You can open a window if'n it gets too hot.

Rich curriculum.

Most courses iz a bunch uv horse manure.

Students represent a broad spectrum uv society.

They iz known criminals attendin this here skool.

The college competes in five sports.

They ain't never had a winnin season.

Most students come frum in-state.

The out-of-state tuition iz sky high.

The library has a hundred en thirty-two thousand, five hundred en forty-two volumes.

If it took you one second to count each book, workin two hours a day, four days a week, makin $3.75 a hour, you would be out uv a job in five weeks en only have $138.75 to show fer it.

The book store, the library, en the administration buildin iz centrally located.

The dorms are on one side uv the campus en the classrooms are way over on the other side uv the campus.

The high-rise dorms all have elevators.

There iz two elevators witch hold four peepul at a time fer three hundred students on twenty floors.

The campus iz spread out over a gently rollin hillside, creatin a stimulatin academic atmosphere.

To go frum your English class to your Math class, it iz five hundred yards: By the Pythagorean Theorem, it iz four hundred yards horizontal en three hundred yards vertical.

The Political Science Department maintains an impartial view uv political ideologies.

They iz a bunch uv communist professors in the political science department.

The Chemistry Department has a wealth uv lab equipment.

The three Bunsen burners that twelve lab students have to share were real expensive.

The college has a very active student guvmint.

Student radicals have taken over the Administration buildin seven times in the last three years.

Small, frendly campus.

The enrollments iz droppin like a rock.

More that 50% uv the graduates go on to graduate skool.

Ain't nobody willin to hire most uv the peepul who graduate frum this here skool.

This skool has an excellent reputation.

This here skool iz one uv the top five hundred skools in the country. It iz not one uv the top four hundred en fifty.

Dorm assignments are made on a lottery system.

Chances are your roommate iz goin to be one er more uv these:

1. *A nose picker.*
2. *A fart blossom.*
3. *The body odor champ on your floor.*
4. *A better cusser than you.*

The dorms are co-ed.

In the dorm you pick, most uv the girls on your floor iz either:

1. *A nose picker.*
2. *A fart blossom.*
3. *The body odor champs on your floor.*
4. *A better cusser than you.*

Well, that's about it on this here end. Take it easy en enjoy the summer.

Oh yeah. Me en Bob got a summer project all lined up. Bob done come acrost a bunch uv my letters in a shoe box, en we iz goin to put them together en make a book!

Your frend forever,

Sherlock

GLOSSARY

a count: account
acrost: across
acuz: because
advenchure: adventure
afore: before
agerculcher: agriculture
ah: I
Ah M fine: I am fine.
Aint: Aunt
allwayz: always
alsew: also
alternate passage burps: farts
ansers: answers
assburns: aspirins
askes: asks
askin: asking
awl: all
Babtist: Baptist
bestest: best
bidness: business
bowkay: boquet
brung: brought
cain't: can't
CoCola: Coca Cola
competishion: competition
condishun: condition

congradulayshuns: congratulations
coulda: could have
count: part of "on a count": on account, because
dansers: dancers
dawg: dog
deboner: debonair
Deer: Dear
dew: do
dickshunerry: dictionary
didunt: didn't
differnt: different
doan't : don't
dominunt: dominant
eleventeen: a large number (usually exaggerated)
em-bare-ussed: embarrassed
emoshunaly: emotionally
en: and
enuff: enough
ennyhow: anyhow
ennyway: anyway
er: or
espeshully: especially
essept: except
ever: every
evenchully: eventually
everbuddy: everybody
exsepshun: exception
ezzampul: example
faverit: favorite
feachures: features
fer: for
figgered: figured

fizzikul: physical
flee: flea
flowerdy: flowery
frend: friend
frum: from
furevvur : forever
git: get
graduwayshun: graduation
grate: great
hambooger: hamburger
hared: haired
haybeus corpses: habeus corpus
herritidge: heritage
history: history
hosbittul: hospital
How R U: How are you
icin: icing
if'n: if
impreshun: impression
impruve: improve
innerduced: introduced
insterments: instruments
itch job: to scratch what itches
iz: is; are
Jackunese: Japanese
Jawjuh: Georgia
kar/kars: car/cars
keybored: keyboard
klukkin: clucking
kuntry: country
Laberdoar: Labrador
lithp: lisp

loo wows: luaus
M: am
mah: my
meen: mean
mountins: mountains
mussels: muscles
naybors: neighbors
newrologist: neurologist
nummer: number
obseshun: obsession
on acuz: because
oppertoonity: opportunity
ouwt: out
own uh kount uv: on account of (i.e., because)
peepul: people
pernounce: pronounce
plane: plain
prolly: probably
prostrate: prostate
puhtaters: potatoes
regler: regular
reperzented: represented
rymed: rhymed
scrunchied: scrunched
sekert: secret
sekertary: secretary
seketerry: secretary
sew: so
Shivverlay: Chevrolet
Shivvy: Chevvy (i.e., Chevrolet)
Shepurd: Sheppard (German Sheppard)
shore: sure

skollership: scholarship
skool: school
socker: soccer
sowed: sewed, sewn
speshully: especially
subject: subject
sum: some
sumbuddy: somebody
surrenge: syringe
thang: thing
thank: think (sometimes)
thankin: thinking
thawt: thought
their: there (sometimes)
theirselves: themselves
there: their (sometimes)
thet: that
they ain't: there is not. there are not.
they iz: there is; there are
thow: throw
thuh: the
thurty: thirty
tooken : took
transmishun: transmission
truk: truck
tung: tongue
tyme: time
U: you
uh nuther: another
uhtached: attached
ukalaylee: ukulele
unconscious: self conscious

uncumfterbul: uncomfortable
unkel: uncle
unmentionables: testicles
unnerstand: understand
uther: other
uv: of
vedgetubels: vegetables
vegtubles: vegetables
vetenaryen: veterinarian
we gone : we're going to
werk: work
wif: with
wimmin: women
witch: which
won: one (sometimes)
wont: want
wonted: wanted
wood: would (sometimes)
woodunt: wouldn't
wuzzunt: wasn't
yeller: yellow
yeller-hared: yellow-haired
yore: your
yoreseff: yourself

ENDNOTES

[1] Aunt Peggy is the wife of Jan's brother Hugh.

[2] Coach Bucha: Bucha is the correct spelling. It is pronounced Boo-ha.

[3] Uncle Buddy is married to Jan's sister Charleen. Buddy is a veterinarian.

[4] Charlton and Roger are Hugh and Peggy's kids, thus Bob and Jan's nephews.

[5] J.B. is Bob's dad. He was a widower for a long time and then married Lois, who had been a widow for a long time.

[6] Charleen is Jan's sister. She is also Florida's first woman veterinarian.

[7] Spencer and Leigh are Charleen and Buddy's kids.

[8] Granny is Jan's mother.

[9] Dr. Hines was Sherlocks veterinarian in Alpharetta.

[10] Aunt Nita is Bob's sister.

[11] Uncle Joe is Bob's older brother. He is married to Bobbye Nann.

[12] Steve is a friend of Bob's he met through his work. Julie is his wife and Stewart is their son. Bob has been to their home many times. They live in Charlotte, NC.

[13] Kady is a paralegal and a friend of Jan's. Trisha is a lawyer and the daughter of Gerry and Isey, some good friends of Bob and Jan's.

[14] Names changed in this story to protect the innocent.

[15] Uncle Gary is Bob's younger brother. Gary is married to Judy.

[16] Holly and Emily are Gary and Judy's daughters, thus Bob and Jan's nieces.

[17] Gerry & Isey are long-time friends of Bob and Jan and Sherlock. Gerry and Bob work together.

[18] Bill and Ellen are friends of Sherlock, Bob and Jan from when they lived in Alpharetta, Georgia.

[19] Malaine is Uncle Joe and Aunt Bobbye Nann's daughter, thus Bob and Jan's niece.

[20] tubin – tubing: floating down the river in inner tubes.

[21] Papa Bruce was a widower for many years. Then he married Granny who had been a widow for many years.

[22] Ginny is Papa Bruce's daughter. Joe is his son-in-law.

[23] Jimmy and Dianne are friends of Sherlock, Bob and Jan from when they lived in Alpharetta, Georgia. Diane is French Canadian; so her name is pronounced Dee Ann; so, of course, that's how Sherlock spells it.

35848408R00132

Made in the USA
Lexington, KY
28 September 2014